The British Horse Society
Riding Class

The British Horse Society
Riding Class

Howell Book House Inc
230 Park Avenue, New York
New York 10169

First published in the United States by
Howell Book House 1986
230 Park Avenue, New York
New York 10169

Published in the United Kingdom by Ebury Press

Note: Throughout this book, American terms and practices
are given in brackets after their British equivalents.

Conceived and produced by
Swallow Publishing Limited
32 Hermes Street, London N1

Editor: **Anne Yelland**
Art director: **Glynis Edwards**
Designer: **Sylvia Tate**
Illustrator: **Coral Mula**
Black and white photography: **Peter Loughran**
Reference photography: **Peter Loughran**
Picture research: **Liz Eddison**
Studio: **Del and Co.**
Articles: **Jane Wilton-Smith**
Consultant: **Susan Giddings**

ISBN 0 87605 860 8

Typeset in Bembo by Typecast, London N16
Printed and bound by Butler and Tanner Ltd, Frome, Somerset, United Kingdom.

Contents

Foreword

This well laid out book is written for the young novice rider and it should prove a valuable complement to practical lessons. It provides simple straightforward advice from the earliest stages and follows a pattern, known to many riders, similar to the Pony Club D, C, and B tests. I personally took this path and can wholeheartedly recommend it.

The practical requirements for looking after a pony are explained and illustrated, and will form the basis for a sensible stable routine. When the rider has progressed sufficiently to want to participate in competitions, advice on how to enter and prepare for an event will be useful for the novice. Finally, the book will help those who may be thinking of careers with horses.

To all riders – good luck and happy landings!

Major Malcolm Wallace
Director General of the British Equestrian Federation and former Chef d'Equipe to the British Olympic Three Day Event Team

These riders are enjoying a ride out on Dartmoor in England. This is one of the best ways to see the countryside around you.

Introduction

Riding Class has been written to give young people from the age of about eight years to sixteen years an idea of horses – both riding them, and training and caring for them. It has not been the authors' intention to set out a definitive work on horsemanship but to offer readers a chance to understand the horse. This book should complement the student's regular riding lessons, and guide him or her through a generally accepted way of working with and handling ponies and horses. It is written for pure pleasure, to enable readers to enjoy their riding and improve their technique. The book gives the reader the opportunity to understand the basic art of riding safely and correctly, to learn about people who have achieved a very high level of riding ability and, perhaps, to follow in their footsteps.

Riding Class looks at every aspect of learning to ride within the framework of the Pony Club and Riding Club tests and grades, from the very first riding lesson through to the Pony Club B test. Riding skills from mounting, and the correct position in the saddle (for both general riding and jumping), the basic paces and jumping, to the techniques necessary for successful eventing, are covered. The book also discusses the basic care of the animal, both stabled and at grass. This is not, however, primarily a book on stable management but should be read in conjunction with lessons at an approved riding school. If you are fortunate enough to own your own animal, the book will be a valuable adjunct to the lessons you receive from qualified trainers when you are working with your own horse or pony. The book sets out to show how much pleasure and enjoyment can be gained from working correctly and safely with horses, both as a hobby and as a possible career.

A high standard in basic care and grooming of your pony and of yourself are essential if you intend to take part in showing classes.

Virginia Holgate Leng
Champion eventer

'When I was young if anyone had told me that one day I would ride the course at Badminton, let alone win it, and be picked for the British Olympic team and gain a silver medal, I just wouldn't have believed them. Looking back over my riding career and remembering the big things I did wrong (the little things are far too numerous to mention), I can see that I owe a great deal to many people in my life.

'To start with, I have always been very grateful to my grandfather who bought a gangly colt at Five Lanes Cattle Market, and gave it to me. The colt was Dubonnet, or Dubby as I soon called him, and he grew up to be my honest friend. I did a lot of learning on him. When I was sixteen Dubby and I entered our first show-jumping class at a local gymkhana. Dubby didn't like the combination towards the end of the course and ran out

three times. We were eliminated. Luckily for me Sally Strachan, elder sister of Clissy Strachan, saw what had happened, decided that the two of us could do with some lessons and told my mother that she would take us on.

'She was a tough teacher and made me slog around eight or nine cross-country courses on foot, telling her and Clissy how I would ride each fence. Then I had to accompany the two sisters to the Boekelo Three-Day Event in Holland as their groom. I hated it, but it gave me the discipline I needed so badly at that age.

'Finally, in 1971, I was allowed to ride in my first Pony Club One-Day Event at Killerton. Once again I failed miserably and was eliminated. Another chance for me to redeem myself as a rider came when Dubby and I were chosen to ride for the Silverton Pony

Club Team. The dressage went well and everything looked fine. Then I blew it all by setting off to jump the first fence in the show-jumping before the bell. Not only was I automatically eliminated for this, but so was the whole team.

'After that, I committed the sin of missing out fences in my first British Horse Society trials and was eliminated. My gloom and despair were immense, so I was delighted to get my first official rosette – for tenth place in a One-Day Event at Wylye. To this day that rosette has pride of place.

'The first Three-Day Event I took part in was in 1972 at Tidworth, where Dubonnet jumped a clear round across country and put me on the shortlist for the Junior European Three-Day Event Championships. What excitement! My mother, who has always been at the helm to steer my career, arranged for Pat Manning to give me lessons.

'The training I received from her was invaluable – I would never have progressed without her help – and Dubby and I won the Junior European Championship in France. Pride always comes before a fall, they say, and it certainly did in my case. After gaining the junior title and thinking myself wonderful, I managed to fall flat on my face, twice, round a simple show-jumping course at Ermington in Devon. That experience humbled me before preparing for my first Badminton in 1974.

'Preparation for Badminton included cross-country schooling at Wylye with Lady Hugh Russell. She had great

11

influence on my ability to see a good line through a combination fence and to keep the horse going straight as I ride through it. She has been an invaluable help to me over many years.

'Pat Manning, Sally and Clissy Strachan and Dorothy Willis (Dot), Pat's head girl, were still helping me, but I'm afraid my first performance at Badminton was not distinguished. After jumping Huntsman's Leap I spent a long time in the bushes, trying to fight my way out, while Richard Meade had time to jump five fences. When I emerged I did manage to complete the course, but I incurred many penalties.

'In 1976, whilst preparing for Badminton again, I fell at Ermington and smashed my left arm in twenty-three places. The doctors thought it might have to be amputated but my mother wouldn't hear of it. Thanks to some very skilful surgery the arm was saved and I managed to ride Tio Pepe at Burghley six months later. Stupidly, I missed out a jump and was eliminated, so now I always walk the show-jumping course of a Three-Day Event at least four times.

'Since those days of making awful, unforgivable mistakes I have, with my wonderful Priceless, had some thrilling successes at the 1982 World Championships, the 1984 Olympics and Badminton 1985. I am well aware that I owe those successes, in great part, to all the people who have helped and encouraged me over the years, not least my mother who has been a constant source of strength. I look forward to going on and successfully riding in many more competitions.'

Vicky Letherbarrow
Show-jumper, age 16

'I come from a farming family, and live in a small Warwickshire village, near to Stratford-upon-Avon. I was brought up with livestock, which included horses and ponies, and started riding at the age of three, on an old Shetland Pony, called Heather. When I wanted to ride, I used to lead Heather alongside a gate in the paddock, climb up the gate and then slide down the pony's neck.

'As children, all four of us were keen members of the Pony Club and local riding club, and some of my ponies were handed down from my elder sister and brother. My sister, Jenny, who is now a veterinary surgeon, passed her Pony Club tests and instructed at P.C. Camp and

rallies; she helped the three of us a lot. We had a lot of fun with some Welsh pony foals, which my parents bought from a sale in Wales. Jenny broke them in and one of them – Paith Blue Peter, a 12.2 hand grey gelding – showed great talent. Really, it was mainly through him that I started in show-jumping. At that time we also did a lot of leading rein gymkhanas – my parents doing the running for me. I started to show-jump with Paith and his companion, Ginger Beer, a roan 12 hand pony, in clear round and 12.2 competitions at the age of five. We then registered Paith with the BSJA and I progressed to affiliated jumping. It was quite a transition from speeding round local classes to the bigger and more demanding BSJA tracks.

'I had an excellent instructress, Mrs Anne Dewey, who had a lot of experience instructing the Pony Club. She taught me about flatwork, and also arranged for me to have some lessons with the late Caroline Bradley. I admired Caroline Bradley a great deal, she was so dedicated and quiet and very good with novices, and I benefited a great deal from her tuition. At the age of seven I qualified and jumped Paith at the Birmingham International Show, and in my last year at 12.2 hands I took him over to Ireland to compete at the Dublin Indoor Show.

'When I was ten, I was chosen to represent England in the 12.2 team at the Home International competitions between England, Ireland, Scotland and Wales. I have been in the English teams every year since with 12.2, 13.2 and now 14.2 hand ponies. I had a tremendous amount of fun with one of my 13.2 ponies called Mystic Star, a grey gelding, who loved jumping and always tried his best for me. Together we won the 13.2 hand BSJA championship and paraded at the Horse of the Year Show.

'My whole day (apart from school) is taken up with ponies. I train on the farm daily. We do all our own work – we don't have grooms or helpers. I feel that it makes for a better relationship with my ponies, doing everything for them and almost living with them. Sometimes I ride out a pony before I catch the school bus which fortunately for me stops at the farm gate! We have an outdoor sand manège and this is where most of the training and schooling is done,

although we do sometimes use the rest of the farm when the weather permits. Sometimes, if the weather is bad, I hack out on the road.

'I spend about 3 to 3½ hours a day schooling and exercising, and perhaps jump the competitive ponies about once a week, as they do not need any more than that. I have always ridden all sorts of ponies, including bringing on novices – I have just broken in and started to jump a young 14.2, which we bred ourselves. I think it makes for a better rider, riding all types and I enjoy doing novices.

'As you have to be so dedicated to succeed, I just do not have time for other sports and hobbies. Earlier I did some running for Warwickshire schools, but had to give it up as I could not devote the time needed to train. My school friends, some of whom ride themselves, are always interested to hear about my show-jumping, and my school staff have always been very interested in my achievements. They are very good about days off for teams and county shows, but I try to keep these to a minimum, as I dislike too much copying up afterwards.

'My most thrilling experience so far was winning the Individual gold medal at the European Pony Championships in Rotterdam last year. I was invited to attend a weekend course at Stephen Hadley's at the last minute, after Miss Tinka Taylor saw me take part in the English 14.2 team at the Wales and West Show. I was then selected with my 14.2 palomino gelding Prince Pepi to travel as reserve to Holland. You can

imagine my delight when I won the Individual gold medal and then gained a place on the British team, which went on to win the gold medal in the team competition. We then went to Brasschaat in Belgium where we won the Nations Cup and I won the Individual Grand Prix and was the leading rider at the show. It was a wonderful experience.

'I have had an awful lot of help with my riding, particularly from my younger sister Charlotte. She took over my 12.2 and 13.2 ponies, when I outgrew them and I taught her the best way to ride them. She also rode them in Home Internationals and the Royal International Horse Show. We worked as a team at home and at shows, as she knew exactly what I needed done. We constructively criticized each other and also lunged each other on the ponies. Sadly, though, Charlotte was tragically killed at the age of 12 years in an accident a few months ago. I miss her very much in everything I do.

'I would very much like to become a professional show-jumper. My parents would be agreeable to this, I know, as they have done so much for me up to now, with my ponies. I shall be out of ponies this year and on to horses in 1987. Anyway, at the moment I am concentrating on qualifying for some of the top competitions and hopefully to be picked for further teams this year, at the same time I am studying for my school exams. My great ambitions are to get a homebred horse to the final of the Foxhunter at Wembley and I hope one day to represent my country in adult classes.'

Horse care and handling

Ponies are unpredictable and sensitive animals. Living wild, they manage to survive almost all the year round without human help, although hay is usually dropped for them during severe winters. If, however, you see ponies and horses in the wild, you will find that they are not as round and plump as those you have probably seen at the various horse shows around the country. This is because the wild pony spends his entire life wandering in search of food, water, and shelter. The privately owned competition pony, on the other hand, will lead a cosseted life, because he will only be successful if he is in good condition.

Wild ponies are suspicious of human beings because they rarely meet them, and the new-born foal of a privately owned pony will be just as sensitive and nervous. Only by careful handling and good treatment will a young foal grow up to trust human beings and be a pleasure to you. Success in handling animals depends on the person dealing with them having endless patience, tact, kindness and firmness, and common sense. It is also important that you are not afraid; a pony will soon realize if you are not sure of yourself. Try to gain his confidence, perhaps with a little food or titbit given by hand (though only give treats in moderation – a pony can learn to demand them and snap in anticipation). When you approach the pony speak to him in an encouraging tone – all animals are susceptible to the tone of the human voice. Do not rush or bustle, any hasty movement will only make a pony nervous.

General handling, leading, grooming and management of a pony are very important and responsible tasks, but it is essential that you learn to do them well. Before you start to think about riding technique, you must be confident around the pony and be able to help care for him. Once he trusts you, he will be calm and unafraid when you are there and be more ready to understand anything new that is required of him.

Water is a major part of a horse's diet. These mares have introduced their foals to a quiet stretch of river so they may drink.

Catching the grass-kept pony

Most average ponies are cared for in the field; for this reason, you should know how to approach and catch a grass-kept animal. Many grass-kept ponies are pleased to have human company and will come to you and be caught very easily. Others, however, find good grass too tempting and prefer to stay out, so it is sensible to assume that the pony would prefer not to be caught. Approach him quietly, talking to him so that you do not surprise him. Have a little food or a titbit in your pocket and keep the headcollar (halter) behind your back so that it is not obvious that you want to bring him in to work. Do not take your saddle and bridle into the field: catch the pony, tie him up and then fetch the saddle and bridle.

Putting on the headcollar

1 Undo the buckle on the near-side cheek-piece of the headcollar. Approach the pony on the near side, and have a feed tin or a little food in your hand, and the headcollar and rope behind your back.

2 Speak to your pony and gain his confidence by letting him have the food, and while he is eating, put your right arm around his neck, and quietly slip the rope around his neck. Slip the noseband of the headcollar over his muzzle.

3 Put the headpiece of the collar over the pony's ears and do up the buckle on the cheek-piece again.

THE HEADCOLLAR
The headcollar is usually made of leather or nylon, and is used for holding or leading the pony, and tying him up. Most consist of a noseband, and throat-lash, which are connected by a short strap, and a headpiece. A buckle on the near-side cheek-piece makes the headpiece adjustable, and easy to put on the pony. The leading rope is usually attached to a ring at the back of the noseband.

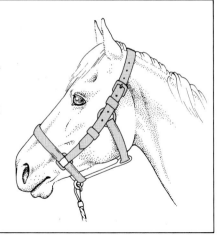

Karen Stives and Ben Arthur at the Los Angeles Olympics, 1984.

Leading the pony

It is best to lead from the near, or left, side of the pony, as he will be used to being handled from this side from an early age. Walk beside him, holding the rope or lead rein near his head in your right hand, and the spare end of the rope in your left hand. Do not pull him or look back. Walk beside his shoulder, say firmly 'Walk on' and encourage him forwards. You should wear gloves so that your hands are protected in case he pulls away from you or takes fright. It is so easy to say that he would not do such a thing, but he may be frightened by something, and the rope could hurt your hands.

A young rider leads her pony in from the field in the correct manner.

Tying up

To groom and care for the pony, he must be 'tied up' with a headcollar and rope to a piece of string. The headcollar must fit the pony properly; if it is too small it will be uncomfortable for him and if it is too large, it could well slip off. The special knot used to tie up ponies is called a 'quick release knot' and is illustrated below. Many stables have a ring to tie the pony to, but it is a good idea to tie a small looped piece of string to the ring, and tie the rope to the string. This will secure the pony but, if he should pull back for any reason, he will break the string, not the headcollar.

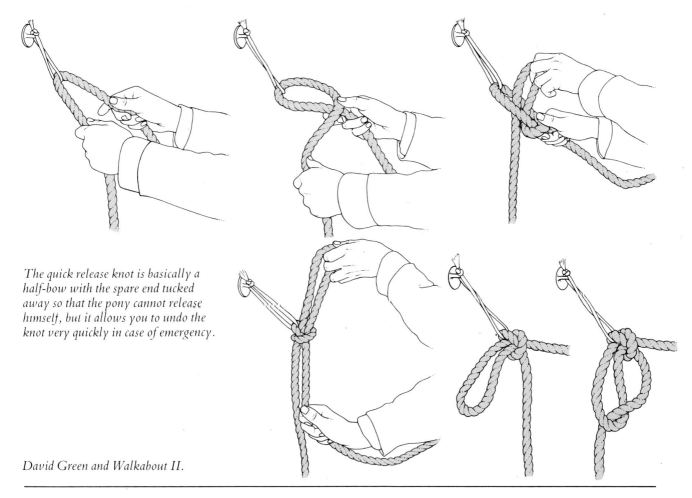

The quick release knot is basically a half-bow with the spare end tucked away so that the pony cannot release himself, but it allows you to undo the knot very quickly in case of emergency.

David Green and Walkabout II.

Horse and pony care

Owning and caring for animals is an enormous responsibility. They are totally dependent upon you for their food, water, health and management, and will need attention every day. Each morning, you must check that your pony has suffered no injuries during the night; that his feet are in good condition, he has not lost a shoe and there are no nails protruding; and that he has eaten all his hay or hard feed. He should have bright eyes and be alert and interested in his surroundings; he should not appear at all dull or depressed.

If you are considering buying your own pony or horse, you must think very carefully about whether to keep him stabled or to care for him 'in the field'. There are advantages to both methods.

Field care

Most ponies are cared for in the field and, in many ways, this is easier than looking after a stable-kept horse. The pony will need about 1.5 hectares (3-4 acres) of good pasture which is well fenced, with no gaps large enough for him to get through. You should also make sure that there are no sharp nails in the fencing that he could cut himself on. All fences should be checked regularly for safety and security.

The field will need some form of shelter − either a purpose-built field shelter, or a high hedge or trees − to protect the pony from the wind and rain in the winter and from flies in summertime.

The pony must have a daily supply of fresh water; if you are fortunate you may have it piped on to the field with an automatic watering system, otherwise you will have to carry it to a tank or trough. Again, check that there are no nails or rivets protruding into the tank, and make sure that it is situated away from any trees − falling leaves will quickly spoil the water. A pond or stream is not sufficient, the pony *must* have access to fresh water.

A pony cannot, however, live continually in the same field. Ponies are fussy eaters and eat only the grasses they like, and the land quickly becomes sour from their droppings. You should remove these daily to preserve the pasture. You must also check the field regularly for litter, for holes, and for weeds − poisonous weeds obviously are harmful to your pony but others will take goodness from the soil. If you are friendly with your local farmer, he may help you to keep the field in good order; it will need to be rolled, harrowed and limed.

The grass first begins to grow in early April and is at its best from mid-May through to June; by early July it is beginning to lose some of its natural goodness. By October, the grass has stopped growing and its food value therefore is not very high, so from then on, through the winter months, you will have to supplement the pony's food with hay and hard feed such as pony cubes (pellets). In really bad weather when there is frost and snow, it is very important to give him more food than usual as the pony will not be able to graze

at all. The trough will be frozen too, so you will have to carry water out to the field every few hours in the daytime.

For these reasons, many people find it better to keep their ponies at grass in the summer and have them part stable kept in the winter. It is easier to care for the pony in the stable in severe winter conditions, and you can still turn him out for a few hours each day for some exercise. The pony will be much warmer in the stable and, consequently, will not need so much food for

warmth or to stay in condition. Although you will have to buy bedding and you will have the additional task of mucking him out (mucking the stall), in the long run he will possibly cost less to keep than when he is shivering out in the field and you are having to give him large amounts of hay and hard feed.

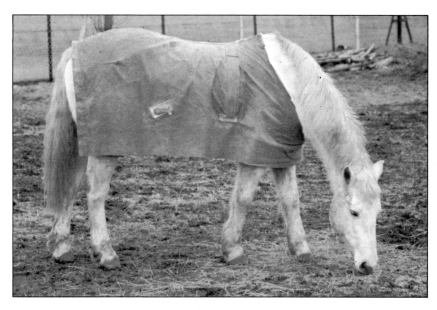

This pony is wearing a correctly fitted New Zealand rug. The fitting is important so that the pony does not become rubbed or sore.

Below: Arab yearlings at play, enjoying one another's company.

Stable care

There are various reasons for having your horse or pony 'stable kept' all the year round. It may be there is a shortage of suitable grazing land, or that it fits in better with your way of life. Your horse or pony may be too finely bred to do well outside, or he may be a fit eventer, racehorse, or show-jumper who needs more sophisticated management and a high protein diet, with little bulk food such as hay.

Many owners find a compromise in the care of the stabled horse by keeping him in at night and turning him out into the field for relaxation for a few hours each day. This is a very good way of caring for show horses and ponies who must look superb in the ring but also have to be very well mannered and relaxed.

Practical daily care

All ponies and horses are by nature creatures of habit and thrive on a regular routine. For this reason, you should adopt a routine which is practical for you to follow, whether you are at school, or on holiday.

7am Go to the stable and check that the pony has suffered no injuries in the night, that he has drunk most of his water, and finished his nightly hay ration. If he is wearing a rug (blanket), adjust it if it has slipped – it could make him sore. Give him fresh water, tie him up and begin the task of mucking out. This is the correct term for the removal of the soiled bedding and droppings. Sweep (rake) the floor clean and put down fresh straw or woodshavings. Give

him a small haynet (say about 1.5kg, 3lb) to munch while you are mucking out. Then tidy up the stable area, put the tools safely away, and give the pony a feed. Untie him, put away the headcollar and rope and leave him in peace to eat his pony cubes, bran and, perhaps, a few oats.

A straw stable being mucked out. This is one of the tasks that has to be performed daily.

Left: Stabled horses must be fed hard food three to four times a day, but hay makes up the majority of their diet, and they require at least two haynets each day.

Now is the time to go and have your own breakfast.
8am If it is a work, or school, day turn the pony out in the field if the weather is good (but not too hot or humid). If not, leave him in the stable with plenty of water and another small haynet. Holidays are much easier to arrange as after you have had your breakfast and made sure that your pony has had at least an hour to digest his, you can go for a ride. The stable-kept horse should be ridden every day, but if this is not possible – say, when you are at school – turn him out in a field for two or three hours at least. If it is a day when you are able to ride, groom the pony (see pages 26-7) before his exercise and again thoroughly afterwards.
12.30pm At lunchtime, remove any droppings from the stable, give the pony fresh water, and then another small hard feed. On school days, you may have to ask someone to do this for you.

4pm Later in the afternoon, clean your saddle and bridle and groom your pony. Make his bed tidy and add extra straw if it is not thick enough for the night.
5.30pm Give the pony his last hard feed with a little hay.
8.15pm Do a last check for the night before you go to bed and give him his main hay.

Naturally, this routine may not suit everyone; you will probably have to adapt these basic rules to suit your way of life. However, so long as you establish a regular routine that will be easy for you to stick to, your pony should thrive.

Stable management is a very important subject and, although it is not the aim of this book to delve into management and care too deeply, you should know a little about them. Later, if you work for your Pony Club tests and Riding Club grades, you will need to know more. Contact your national riding organization, or ask your instructor, for a list of books.

THE BASIC RULES

1 Check every day for injuries; check shoes, feet and general health and condition.
2 Establish a regular routine which is practical for you to follow easily.
3 Give your pony plenty of fresh water, and always water him before you feed him.
4 Do not ride for at least an hour after the pony has had a feed.
5 Make sure his bed is a thick cover over the entire floor, so that it encourages him to lie down and sleep without risk of injury.
6 Groom him every day.

Tools for grooming

You will need the following tools to groom your pony:

Two sponges (1), one for cleaning the eyes and muzzle, one for cleaning the dock.

A dandy brush (2) for removing surplus mud and sweat from his coat. This is a stiff brush so it is not suitable for a very fine-skinned animal.

A metal curry comb (3) is used to remove hairs and dirt from the body brush to keep it clean.

A rubber curry comb (4) is used for removing caked mud.

A water brush (5), used wet, helps to lay the mane and damp the top of the tail to keep it in shape.

The stable rubber (6) is used to put a final polish on the coat.

A hoof pick (7) for cleaning mud and stones out of the feet.

A comb (8) for the mane.

A body brush (9) to help give a good shine to the coat, and to brush the mane and tail.

It is important to keep your grooming kit clean and in good repair. Naturally, if your kit is dirty, then your efforts at grooming will be rather pointless. The best way to clean it is to wash the brushes once a week in a bowl of warm water to which you have added a tablespoon of salt. Some ponies' skins are rather sensitive and they can be allergic to soap, so if you use one, choose with care. Finally, try not to get the wooden handles wet, as this will make them rot eventually.

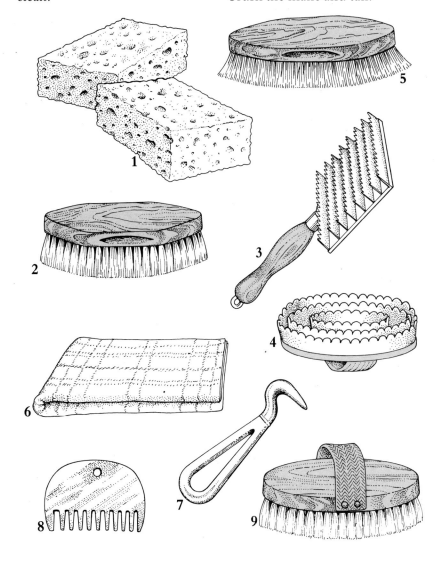

When to groom

It is important for your pony's health, and appearance, that you groom him before you ride. Although you might not mind riding a dirty pony, it is not wise. Mud around his face will be uncomfortable and perhaps dangerous, and dirt under the saddle may rub him and make him sore. You must also pick out (pick) his feet carefully, checking particularly for stones which could bruise him when you are riding.

The pony will also need grooming after exercise, since this is when he is warm and his pores are open. The grass-kept pony will only need brushing off, but make sure that any sweaty areas are completely clean and dry, then put on more fly repellent if the weather is warm. The stable-kept horse or pony, on the other hand, is probably working harder and needs to be really clean and fit, so give him a thorough grooming.

PARTS OF THE PONY

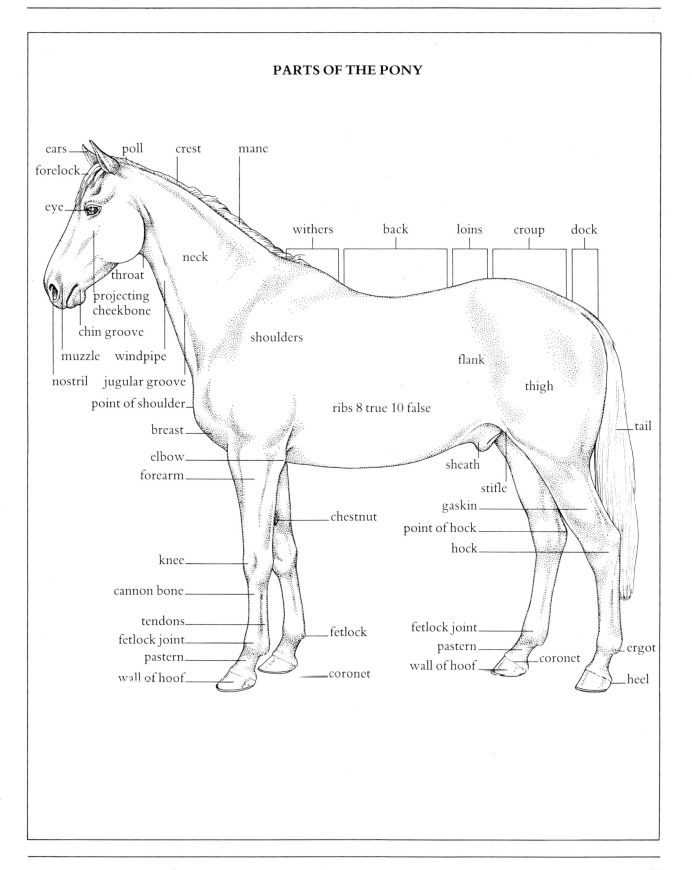

ears — poll — crest — mane
forelock
eye
withers — back — loins — croup — dock
neck
throat
projecting cheekbone
chin groove
muzzle — windpipe
nostril — jugular groove
point of shoulder
breast
elbow
forearm
shoulders
flank
thigh
ribs 8 true 10 false
tail
sheath
stifle
gaskin
point of hock
hock
chestnut
knee
cannon bone
tendons
fetlock joint
pastern
wall of hoof
fetlock
coronet
fetlock joint
pastern
wall of hoof
coronet
ergot
heel

Grooming

Grooming is essential to keep your pony clean, healthy and in good condition and, of course, for his appearance.

The grass-kept pony does not require such thorough grooming as the fit stable-kept horse so we will look at grooming a grass-kept pony first. This should take you about 20 minutes.

First tie up your pony with a well-fitting headcollar and rope to a piece of string attached to a stable ring. Collect your grooming kit; it is a good idea to have a bucket or bag to keep it in so that no articles get lost. Start on the near side and lift one of the feet, then with the hoof pick remove any stones or mud. Work from the direction of the heel towards the toe. Have a skep or bucket to put underneath each foot so that the mud falls into the container and not on to the ground (or the stable floor if you are working inside). Pay particular attention to cleaning the feet of a grass-kept pony, since he is very likely to have stones lodged in them. If the hair over his hoofs is very long, it will need trimming. Comb the hairs upwards then snip them off with scissors. Once a week, brush the hoofs with hoof oil.

Once you have removed the dirt from each hoof, start on the coat. Use the dandy brush and, again starting on the near side, brush the hair with firm sweeps to remove all the mud and dirt. On the near side of the pony, have the brush in your left hand and on the off (right) side of the pony, have the brush in your right hand. Rest your free hand on the pony's back. Keep close to him so that you can feel any

movement he makes, or if he becomes upset in any way. It is always safer to be close in to the pony where you will only be pushed than to stand back and receive the end of a kick.

If your pony has a very hairy coat, you may not need to use the body brush, but you should groom a summer coat especially well with the body brush and curry comb. This time, have the body brush in your left hand and the curry comb in your right hand when you are working on the left side, and vice versa when you are working on the right

side. The body brush is also used to do the pony's head. When you are working around the head, be more gentle, and remember to untie the pony so that he does not become anxious and pull back or shy. Put one hand on his head, and use the other to brush.

Groom the mane and tail with the body brush; both split easily if they are roughly treated, so never use the dandy brush. It is refreshing for the pony to have his eyes, nose and dock sponged and it is also a good idea in summer to go over his coat every day with a fly repellent.

The stable-kept pony does not need as much of the natural oil in his coat to protect him from the elements as the grass-kept pony does so you can give him a more thorough grooming of about half an hour at a time. The routine should follow the same basic pattern as for the grass-kept animal, but grooming with the body brush is very important for the stable-kept pony. This is the way to get him really clean, and it also helps to develop his muscle tone. The stable rubber gives a final polish to the grooming.

Grooming the pony's head is done using the body brush.

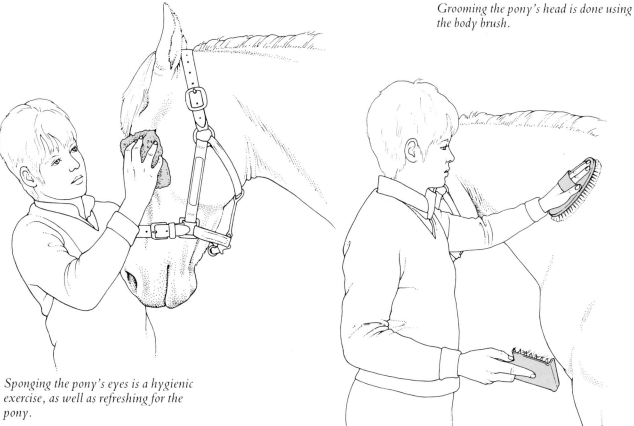

Sponging the pony's eyes is a hygienic exercise, as well as refreshing for the pony.

Picking out your pony's feet every day is very important. Notice how the hoof pick is used in a downward motion from the heel to the toe.

The stable-kept pony is given a thorough grooming using the body brush in conjunction with a curry comb.

Clothes for riding

The different clothes worn by riders in the various disciplines are based on practicality for the situation, and etiquette.

As a beginner, the most important factor is for you to be safe, so you need a strong pair of shoes with leather soles, a heel and no buckles. Training shoes are not suitable because they do not have a heel – without one, your foot could slip through the stirrup. You should also have jeans (preferably stretch) or jodhpurs. Tracksuit bottoms are really too loose – they could rub you and make you sore. You will also need a shirt or sweater, an approved safety hat with chinstrap, and gloves.

This casual dress will be suitable when you first start learning to ride, but as you progress and wish to enter competitions, it will no longer be acceptable. The competition rider wears different clothes for different occasions.

Show-jumper Long leather boots, white breeches, white shirt, white tie (choker), tweed jacket for novice classes, black or red jacket for open classes, approved safety hat with chinstrap

Event rider Cream or fawn breeches, leather boots, hunting tie (stock), navy blue jacket, shirt, skullcap – coloured silk for cross-country

Dressage rider White breeches, top boots, top hat, swallow-tail coat for advanced classes, hacking jacket for novice classes

Showing Hacking jacket for novice classes, navy blue jacket for open classes

Side-saddle Complete habit, boots, shirt, tie or hunting stock, bowler or top hat and veil

CORRECT

INCORRECT

Left: These two photographs show the right and wrong ways to dress if you wish to ride. Starting with the hats, the girl is wearing a riding hat which is correctly secured by a harness. The boy's hat fits badly, and cannot be secured firmly with just a piece of elastic. The girl is wearing a shirt and tie, hacking jacket, gloves, jodhpurs and jodhpur boots, all of which is correct and safe. The boy could ride in an open-necked shirt but has nothing to protect his arms and hands should that be necessary; his

CHOOSING A RIDING HAT

For many years, there has been an enormous choice of riding hats. In 1986, however, the Pony Club, the British Horse Trials Group, the British Horse Society and the United States Combined Training Association, ruled that all competitors in events organized by them must wear a skullcap with chinstrap as worn by racing jockeys (top photograph) or a velvet hard hat with a flexible peak and chinstrap (centre).

At present for dressage competitions, showing, and side-saddle riding, silk top hats, velvet hard hats and bowlers are still permissible. Certainly it would take from the elegance of side-saddle riding if a cross-country skullcap was used! Show-jumpers must wear a hard hat, and are advised to use one with a chinstrap; this is not, however, compulsory in Great Britain (it is for juniors in the United States) at present. Whichever type of hat you choose, make sure that it fits properly. A loose hat (bottom photograph) will give you no protection at all.

As more and more young riders start to take part in competitions in which skullcaps are compulsory, it is to be hoped that they will become so used to wearing these hats that it will be normal for them to use this type of hat for all activities. Remember that you only have one head – make sure you protect it with a properly fitted hat.

CORRECT

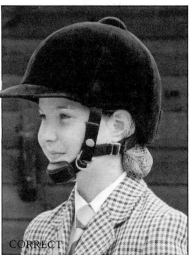

CORRECT

INCORRECT

trousers are loose and baggy, and his legs could become badly rubbed and sore. His shoes are soft and have no heel. He could be hurt if his pony stepped on him, and shoes with no heel mean that his foot could slip through the stirrups.

Above: A correctly turned out group of riders taking part in a showing competition.

Tack

Tack is the name given to the saddlery that the pony wears; this includes the saddle and the bridle. It is important for both your safety and the pony's comfort that the saddlery you use is in excellent condition and perfectly clean. How to care for your saddlery is described on pages 88-9.

For everyday use, an ordinary snaffle bridle is sufficient, though a double bridle is sometimes necessary for the show ring or in some dressage classes (this does not apply in the United States). The saddle should be a general-purpose saddle. This means that it is suitable for simple dressage riding and also for learning to jump. It is not until you begin to specialize in different classes that you need specialist saddles.

The general-purpose saddle should be made of good-quality leather – if you are buying your own, get the best you can afford – and must be neither too big nor too small. If it is over-sized, it may press on the pony's loins and could damage his kidneys, or it may ride up on to his neck. If it is too small, it may pinch the pony and give him a painful pressure mark. The weight of the saddle should rest on either side of the pony's spine – not on the spine itself, or on his withers. In fact, you should be able to see a clear channel from the wither through to the cantle. The saddle must be centrally balanced, with a deep seat. This will encourage you to sit in the correct position.

The different parts of the saddle and bridle are illustrated on page 51.

Putting on the saddle

When you first start riding lessons, it is very likely that your pony will be prepared and tacked up for you. It is, however, good to know how to do this yourself, since it will help you to get used to handling the pony.

1 Put a headcollar on the pony and tie him up as described on pages 16 and 19, then remove his rugs. Pick up your saddle, and approach the pony on the near side, talking to him as you do so to reassure him.

2 Place the saddle on the pony's back near the withers and slide it back into position. It is best to slide it back in this way so that you can be sure that the hairs on the pony's back are lying smooth and flat underneath the saddle and will not be uncomfortable for him.

3 Attach the girth loosely and pull the buckle guards over the buckles of the girth. Gradually tighten the girth; it must be firm so that the saddle does not slip, but be careful not to pinch the pony. You should be able to slide the flat of your hand under the girth, but feel a little pressure against it. Then, lower the stirrup irons.

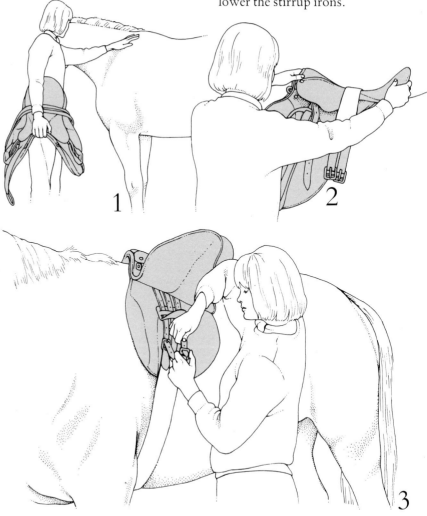

To remove the saddle

Once you have dismounted (see page 34), run the stirrups up the leathers so there is no risk of them injuring the pony, and then put the pony into the stable. There, undo the girth on the near side, go round to the off side (this is the correct term for the right-hand side of the pony) and put the girth over the top of the saddle. Be particularly careful that the buckles do not scratch the leather seat. Return to the near side and lift off the saddle. Massage the pony's back for a few minutes to improve the circulation and then put the saddle away safely so that it does not fall and break the tree (this is the correct term for the 'backbone' of the saddle).

Putting on the bridle

1 Hold the bridle level with the pony's head to check it is fitted at approximately the correct length.

2 With your right hand holding the bridle at the headpiece, open the pony's mouth with your left hand and slip the bit into his mouth.

3 Fit the headpiece and the browband over the pony's head so that you can arrange the complete bridle, and do up the throat-lash. Allow the full width of your hand between the throat-lash and the side of the pony's jaw-bone.

4 Fasten the noseband, allowing two fingers' width between the band and the pony's face, and check that the bridle is secure.

Mounting

Before you start learning to ride, you must master mounting. This is the term used to describe getting on to your pony's back, and there is a proper and safe way to do this.

1 The pony must stand squarely on all four feet. Stand by his left shoulder, facing his tail, take the reins into your left hand, and with your right hand turn the stirrup iron.

2 Put your left foot into the stirrup iron, making sure that your toe is downwards, then, still holding the reins, put your left hand on to the pony's withers.

3 Put your right hand on the far side of the saddle.

4 When your instructor gives the command to mount, bend your right knee and spring up, swinging your leg over the pony's back.

5 Then, settle yourself lightly into the saddle.

The rider's position

The rider's position in the saddle is the basis and foundation of all future work. Consequently, it is important from your very first lessons that you try hard to

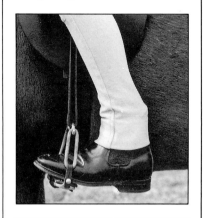

CORRECT STIRRUP

The stirrup leather should be at right angles to the ground, and your heel slightly below the level of your toes. The safety stirrup ensures that if you fall off, your foot will come out of the stirrup so that there is no risk of your being dragged along the ground.

INCORRECT

If your heel is too low, or the stirrup leather too long, you will not get the support or balance your legs need.

maintain as correct a position as possible. From this, you will develop strength, balance and suppleness – you will also feel more secure on your pony.

Once you have mounted, sit in the centre and lowest part of the saddle, with your weight evenly distributed over your two seat bones and your crotch. Your hips should be parallel to those of the pony, your shoulders square, and your elbows bent loosely in to your sides. Your upper arm should form almost a right-angle to your forearm, and your fingers should be closed around

the rein. Make sure that your heels are below the level of your toes and the stirrup leathers are set at a comfortable length. The lower part of your leg should hang loosely by the weight of the leg alone to the barrel of the pony, and the inside part of your leg should be in a position to be applied calmly and firmly as an effective aid when you need it. Finally, keep your head up – you should be able to picture an imaginary vertical line from your ear through your shoulder, hip and heel, and a horizontal line from the bit to your hand.

Dismounting

As we have seen, there is a correct and safe way to mount. The same is true when you want to get down from your pony. The illustrations below show how to dismount on the left side of the pony; eventually, however, you should be able to dismount from either side.

1 Sit upright, facing forward, and take both feet out of the stirrups.

2 Put the reins into your left hand and put your right hand on the pony's withers. You use your right hand to give you the push you need to swing off.

3 Swing your right leg over the pony's back. As you do so, move your left hand to the withers to take your weight. Make sure that you do not catch the pony with your foot as you swing it over.

4 Land with your knees bent. Run the stirrup irons up the leathers before you lead your pony away.

HOW TO HOLD THE REINS

Settle yourself in the basic position, with your elbows bent and loose in to your sides. Take a rein in each hand, placing it between your third and little fingers, across your palm, and over your index finger. Your thumb should rest on top, and your palms face each other.

Always remember that there should be a straight line from your elbows, through your hands to the pony's mouth, so that when the pony bobs his head up and down, your hands and elbows must move to keep the line.

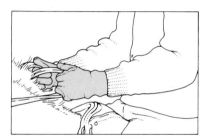

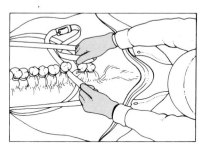

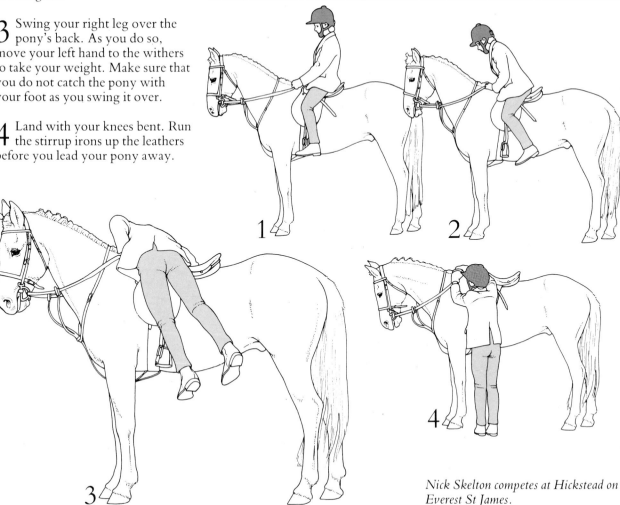

Nick Skelton competes at Hickstead on Everest St James.

The aids

The aids are the main means of communication between you and your pony – it is through them that you convey your wishes to the pony. The importance of giving clear and effective aids will become obvious when we look at the basic paces. There are several aids, but basically they can be divided into two types: natural and artificial. The natural aids are your legs and weight, your voice and, through the reins, your arms.

The artificial aids are whips and spurs. The whip is used to reinforce your leg aids when the pony does not respond to your leg. It must not be used to punish your pony. There is no hard and fast rule about which hand to carry your whip in – common sense is the best guide. Your teacher will probably tell you to start with it in your inside hand, but you should be prepared to change hands as and when you need to. To change a short riding whip (no longer than 70cm, 27in.) from one hand to the other, first put both reins into one hand. You must do this first, so that you do not lose control of your pony at any point. Then, pass the whip through to your other hand, over the pony's withers, and separate the reins again.

Spurs give a more refined aid. Because you could hurt your horse or pony through the incorrect use of spurs, they should not be used until you have a truly independent lower leg position (see page 83).

In the use of the aids, you must learn to develop the co-ordination to use your legs and hands independently of each other. In many sports – tennis, for example, or gymnastics – the sportsman uses his arms and legs together to balance the rest of his body. You cannot do this when you are riding as it would muddle and confuse your pony.

To handle the reins well, learning to become independent of them for your balance, takes time and practice. Work on the lunge line (which we will look at on pages 40-1) will help you to develop a seat independent of the reins. You may have heard the expression 'good hands'; this does not mean that they are supple and attractive, but that they are sympathetic and effective, able to give signals to the pony necessary for precision and control, without the rider losing balance in any way or at any time.

Far left: Tanya Larrigan-Robinson and Salute.

The rider has gained the horse's attention at the halt and is now preparing to give a further aid to move the horse forward into his work.

The basic paces

The picture that you make on your pony should be one of relaxation and confidence, which will only come with practice. We have already stressed the importance of sitting correctly on your pony (or establishing a good seat). One of the best ways to do this is by work on the lunge. For this reason, your first riding lessons will probably be on the lunge line, although if you start riding when you are very young, or if you are a little nervous, the lead rein is more suitable.

The lead rein allows your instructor to walk alongside you, talking to you and building your confidence, while at the same time correcting the faults in your basic position. In this way, you will begin to feel the pony's movements and develop the fluid balance to follow them without being stiff or tense. Progress on the lead rein is often slower than work on the lunge, but it is ideal for very small riders. Over the age of about six, it is probably better to start on the lunge line.

The lunge is a long lead rein. Your instructor stands at one end, and you sit on your pony at the other, and, usually, ride around in a circle. Lungeing is an excellent way to improve the balance and security of your seat – indeed, even experienced riders go back to lunge work. By allowing you to concentrate on what you are doing without worrying too much about controlling your pony, lunge lessons also help you build up your confidence. Another advantage of the lunge is that the pony can be worked through all paces – walk, trot and canter – on it; this means that you have time to become used to the movement of the pony, and to work on the correct position at all paces. Once you know that you can sit correctly, and have done some exercises at all paces, you will feel confident enough to start to control the pony yourself through the basic paces.

Young riders often start riding lessons on the lead rein, then progress to lunge lessons. As they become more confident, they will be asked to perform various exercises on the lunge.

Work on the lunge

Work on the lunge is excellent at any stage of your training. It is the best way to improve your seat and correct any positional faults that may occur, since you have only to concentrate on what you are doing, while your teacher controls the pony and watches you to analyse and correct faults as soon as they happen. We have already seen how important it is to sit straight and deep in the saddle and lunge work will help you to perfect this. It is also an excellent way to improve your balance. Lungeing is, however, very strenuous and may make you tired and perhaps a little stiff and sore. Do tell your teacher if you are getting tired –

if your muscles become tense, it is impossible to make progress. Twenty minutes on the lunge is long enough in the early lessons, and 40 minutes maximum time when you are fit.

When you are riding on the lunge, you will make most progress by working without stirrups, although your teacher will probably watch you ride with reins and stirrups first as this will allow him to see how you sit naturally. The teacher will then take your stirrups away and make you hold the front of the saddle lightly with both hands. This will ensure that you are sitting straight with your shoulders and hips level.

Work on the lunge usually begins at the walk, and if this goes well and you look fairly relaxed then your teacher will progress on to sitting trot. You must try to sit still, following the movements of the pony as closely as possible, but still maintaining good balance and rhythm. Transitions can also be practised on the lunge, and your instructor will watch to see whether you are able to stay with the movement of the pony throughout. When your teacher is satisfied, then you may begin work without holding the front of the saddle. This really will test your ability to balance on your pony through all the paces.

Exercises on the lunge

As your confidence grows and balance improves on the lunge, then there are physical exercises which you can do to strengthen and further improve your seat. Make sure that you are sitting in the correct position and in balance on your pony, before you start to move, and do not be tempted to exercise for too long at a time – you will quickly become stiff and tired, rather than supple.

1 Sit in the centre of the saddle, without stirrups, with both hands holding the front of the saddle. This exercise ensures that your hips and shoulders are square to your pony.

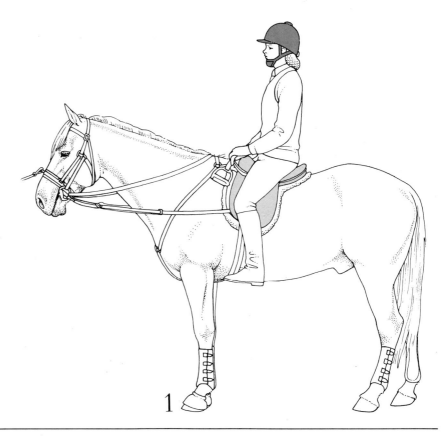

1

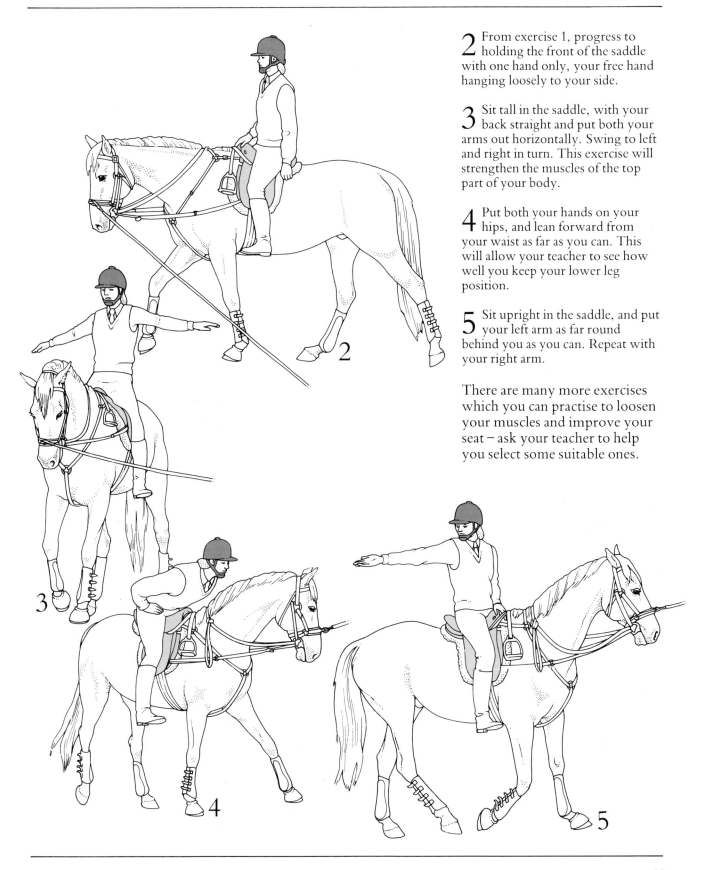

2 From exercise 1, progress to holding the front of the saddle with one hand only, your free hand hanging loosely to your side.

3 Sit tall in the saddle, with your back straight and put both your arms out horizontally. Swing to left and right in turn. This exercise will strengthen the muscles of the top part of your body.

4 Put both your hands on your hips, and lean forward from your waist as far as you can. This will allow your teacher to see how well you keep your lower leg position.

5 Sit upright in the saddle, and put your left arm as far round behind you as you can. Repeat with your right arm.

There are many more exercises which you can practise to loosen your muscles and improve your seat – ask your teacher to help you select some suitable ones.

Walking

Before you are able to ride well at the walk – or the trot or canter – it is important for you to understand what actually happens to the pony in each pace.

There are four steps to make one stride of the walk, and for this reason, the walk is called a pace of four-time. The pony's legs move separately in a marching pace, one after another, in the sequence near-hind, near-fore, off-hind, off-fore. The pony's main balance points are his head and neck and his head will naturally bob up and down in the walk; you therefore must not restrict this movement in any way, otherwise you will upset your pony's balance.

Riding at the walk

You must try to maintain a correct position in the saddle, sitting tall, straight and still in the centre and lowest part. Remember the straight lines through your ear, shoulder, hip and heel, and from the bit through the rein to your hands (see page 33). Your elbows should hang loosely to your

In these photographs the pony is at walk. Notice that the rider's hands have given to allow the pony's head and neck to move forward and down, then up and back. This happens with every stride the pony takes at walk. The rider must never restrict this movement because the pony's stride would shorten and walk would not be free.

sides, neither in front of the body nor behind, and remember to keep your heels below the level of your toes.

Take up the rein contact so that you can just feel your pony's mouth. Look forward and use both of your legs together, nudging your pony's sides. If he does not respond, then nudge him again with your legs, and follow this with a tap with your whip behind your leg. As soon as the pony moves forward, lighten your rein contact a little to allow him to bob his head up and down.

Your legs should work alternately, so as the left foreleg comes back toward you, you must give the pony a nudge on his side with your left leg, and as the right one comes back, you should nudge with your right leg. This will encourage your pony to make a better step with his hindlegs. In this way, your legs will pick up the rhythm and the movement of the walk.

The trot

The trot is a pace of two-time, which means that the pony's legs move in diagonal pairs. The combination of near-hind and off-fore is called the 'right diagonal', and the off-hind and the near-fore the 'left diagonal'. The pony should move with calm, even strides at all times. There are two types of trot: rising (posting) and sitting. Rising trot is a more comfortable pace for hacking out, once you have learned how to do it correctly. Sitting trot, although more tiring, is used when you are changing pace, either lengthening or shortening your stride, and for dressage. This is because you are closer to your pony in sitting trot, and can apply your aids more clearly and effectively.

Riding at a trot

Establish a good walk, your pony must be moving forward with energetic strides. Take up the rein contact so that the reins are slightly shorter than when you ride at the walk; this is because the pony's head will be a little higher than at the walk. Close both legs together and remain sitting in the saddle – your pony will then trot forward. If your pony is a little lazy, you may need to vibrate your leg several times against his sides so that he knows to trot forward. Always move forward into sitting trot for a few strides before commencing rising trot as in this way you are closer to the pony and your signals are clearer.

The rising trot

At a rising trot, you sit in the saddle on one diagonal and rise in the saddle on the other.

Initially, you will probably find it difficult to keep the rhythm and you will bounce and bump in the saddle and find the trot rather tiring and uncomfortable. For this reason, it is better to start on the lunge line or on the lead rein so that you develop a little feel and balance for the movement of the pony. If you are on a lead rein alongside someone who already rides, your teacher can tell you when to sit and when to rise. This will quickly help you to develop the rhythm and learn how to absorb the movement of the pony

through your hip and knee. Once you have mastered rising trot, you will do it effortlessly and wonder why it was a problem in the beginning.

The sitting trot

The sitting trot is a very bumpy pace initially, and it will take time for you to be able to relax, sit still and follow the movements of the pony closely. It is really worth while working to develop a good tall and central position in the saddle at sitting trot, because you will be using the pace so much in the future.

The best way to practise is without your stirrups, preferably on the lunge line.

In these two photographs, the pony is working in trot. This pace is faster than the walk, and may be performed sitting or rising. That means that the rider either remains seated all the time (sitting trot), or that he can rise up and then sit again on every alternate stride (rising trot).

The canter

The canter is a pace of three-time; this means that there are three definite steps to make one stride of canter. For canter right, the first step to leave the ground is the left hindleg. This is followed by the left diagonal (the left foreleg and the right hindleg together), and finally by the right foreleg. The right foreleg is called the leading leg.

Riding at the canter

Your position in the saddle is the same as at the walk, and sitting trot; you must try to sit still and follow the pony's movements closely. You will find that canter is a very comfortable pace, and once you have got used to the faster pace, it is very enjoyable. To canter, you should first ride at the sitting trot. A highly trained animal can go into canter from walk, but when you first start to canter, it is better for you to apply the aids from the sitting trot.

Make sure that your legs are sending the pony forward energetically – he must have plenty of impulsion – then, place your inside leg on the girth and your outside leg behind the girth. Hold the reins so that you can just feel the pony's mouth with the outside rein. Bend the pony slightly to the inside so that you can just see his eye, and with your outside leg give him an extra nudge to tell him to go into the canter; at the same time, keep your inside leg at the girth to keep him moving forward.

The canter is the last of the three paces which the rider has to learn. The transition from trot to canter, and then returning to trot from canter is quite difficult to achieve, as it feels ungainly and may unbalance the rider. This is because the order in which the horse uses his legs changes quickly, and the rider often finds it difficult to adjust from a two-time pace to a pace of three-time.

To slow down or halt

At all times, the pony must pay attention to the rider's aids, especially when he is being asked to slow down or halt.

At whatever pace you are riding, sit still and straight in the saddle, and close both your legs lightly to the pony's sides. Resist a little with your hands (that is, shorten the reins) and then soften the reins (give with them). Your pony should then stop, although obviously this depends on the pace that you are in and your pony's obedience. You may have to resist again with your hands until the pony understands that you wish him to stop.

To make a turn

When you are making any turn, it is important that you look to the direction of the turn. In this way your body and your weight will be in the direction that you intend to go and this will make it easier for your pony to oblige.

The secret of riding a good turn or circle is to prepare early and think the movement before you ask your pony to do it. Make sure that your thought, therefore, becomes your first aid.

To turn right, sit tall in the saddle, and prepare the pony to turn right by positioning him to the right. Look to the right, then place your right leg at the girth and your left leg behind the girth. Pull (resist) on the right rein so that you can just feel the pony's bit. This will bend his head slightly to the right, so you must also remember to give sufficiently with the left rein to allow his head to move this way.

All turns and circles are based on these simple aids.

When asking the pony to turn at any pace, it is most important to keep the rhythm to help maintain balance.

Transitions

Transitions is the name given to all changes of pace, from walk to trot, trot to canter, canter to trot and trot to walk, and of direction.

Transitions are important at all paces and it is well worth practising them until you are able to ride them accurately and at the same time maintain rhythm and balance. They form the basis of almost all lessons, and your ability to ride simple turns and transitions is the foundation of all the more advanced riding you will do later on when preparing for Pony Club tests or Riding Club Grades and when you start competitive riding.

The secret of a good transition is preparation – give yourself plenty of time to think. Prepare by sitting still and tall in the saddle, close both legs to re-balance the pony and resist a little with your hands (take on the reins). This movement, which will get his attention, is called a half-halt, Once you have his attention, you can tell him what to do next. If you want him to go faster, nudge him strongly with your legs, but soften the reins (give a little). Your hands, through the reins and the bit in the pony's mouth, control and receive the energy and impulsion produced by your legs. At the same time, your hands are directing and controlling the head, neck and shoulders of the pony, while your legs create the impulsion and power in his hindquarters.

The hands have three main functions: they act, resist and yield. A good rule is that your hands should never work before your legs; your legs are always used to create impulsion, to give confidence and assist in the balance of the pony.

These ponies and riders competing in the Prince Philip Cup are turning at speed and in balance.

The Pony Club and Riding Club Movement

The main aim of the Pony Club and its various affiliated bodies around the world, and the Riding Club Movement – which in many areas forms a junior branch (chapter) – and its international equivalents is to encourage horse and pony owners to increase their knowledge of riding and stable management for the benefit of both horse and rider.

The greater your technique and skill in any sport, the more you will be able to get out of it. For this reason, branches of the Pony Club and Riding Club hold lectures, demonstrations, training days and competitions and offer riders any advice they may need. They also encourage their members to work for the Pony Club tests and Riding Club grades, and to progress through them so that they gain a thorough knowledge of stable management and horse care, alongside their training in riding and jumping.

The Pony Club D test

The work that we have covered so far will take you comfortably through the Pony Club D test and Riding Club Grade I in most countries. In particular, for this test you must be able to mount and dismount correctly. It is important also that you are able to maintain a correct position in the saddle, so you will be asked to demonstrate how you sit at the slow paces of walk and trot. Before presenting yourself for your test, you must also be able to ride off the leading rein. If you have regular riding lessons, your teacher will not suggest that you take this test until you are confident to ride and manage your pony without being led.

Children taking the D test are usually about eight or ten years old, though naturally if you started to learn to ride when you were a little older, age does not matter at all. The important thing is that, by this first stage, you are discovering that riding is fun, and that you are keen to learn more and improve. If you practise hard, you will progress quickly towards the next grade.

You will not be expected to be able to look after your pony on your own at this level, but you should know a little about him, and about how to approach and handle him, so read the advice on pages 16 and 19. You must also show that you are able to lead him, and to name some simple points of the pony (see page 25) and his saddle and bridle.

Young riders being examined for their D test – the first Pony Club certificate.

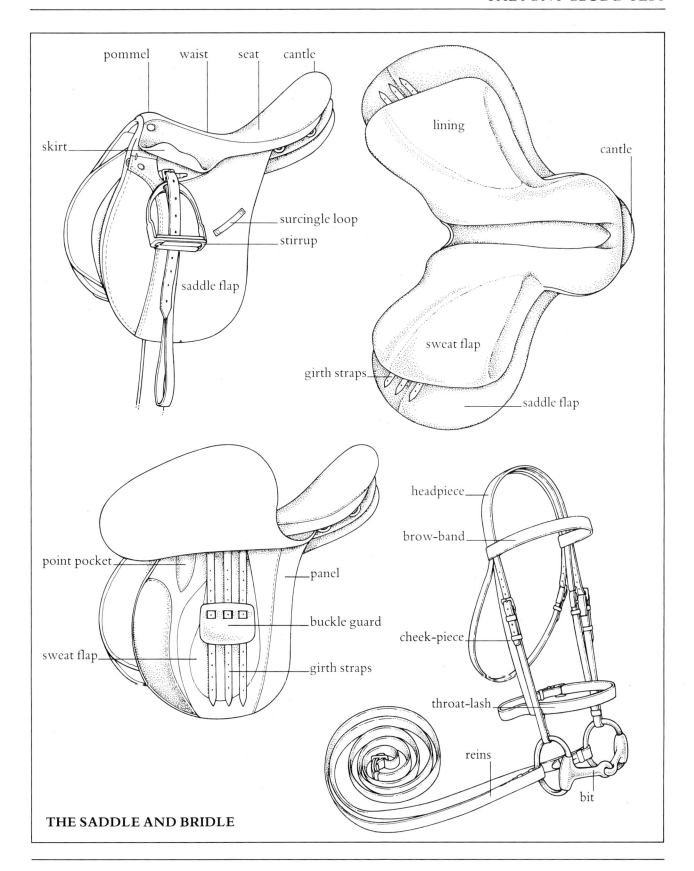

pommel waist seat cantle

skirt

lining

cantle

surcingle loop
stirrup

saddle flap

sweat flap

girth straps

saddle flap

point pocket

panel

buckle guard

sweat flap

girth straps

headpiece

brow-band

cheek-piece

throat-lash

reins

bit

THE SADDLE AND BRIDLE

Road safety

If you are going to be hacking out on the road (trail riding), you must be safe. The Pony Club in Great Britain and in other countries (although not in the United States) holds road safety tests, aimed to help you be more aware of how to conduct yourself when riding on the road, and you should not be allowed to ride out on the road alone until you have passed one of these tests.

You will be tested on your ability to control your pony under all circumstances. The examiner will also check that your saddlery fits properly and is in good repair (cleaning and caring for saddlery are described on pages 88-9) and that your pony has properly fitting shoes that are not dangerously worn (see pages 66-7). You will then be examined on your knowledge of the Highway Code, and be asked to prove your ability in an enclosed area or field. If the examiner is satisfied, you will be asked to perform the road test. Most riding schools and pony clubs now run training courses for road safety tests and you would be wise to take a course so that you can practise under supervision.

Here are a few hints to help you to ride in safety when you are out on the road.
1 Know the Highway Code.
2 Never take young or traffic-shy ponies on the road.
3 Always be courteous, raise your hand to thank all cars that slow down for you.
4 Wear light-coloured clothing so that you can be seen.
5 Give clear hand signals.
6 Avoid going on the roads at night. If you are forced to do so, make sure that an adult with a car travels behind you.

Lucinda Green and Beagle Bay at Badminton, 1983.

It is very important that riders learn to obey the rules of the road if they are going to hack out.

Hacking

Riding away from the security of the riding school, or the field (ring) where you have been learning, is essential for your advancement, but do not start hacking until you are very confident in the field and can really control the pony independently of your instructor. Hacking is a very pleasant experience and the most marvellous way to see the countryside, but your pony must be safe, obedient and as reliable in traffic as he is in open spaces.

Riding in large open spaces and across uneven terrain is an ideal way for you to improve the balance, depth and security of your seat. Initially you should ride mainly at the walk and trot, but as you become more confident you can canter along suitable tracks and bridleways. Avoid ground that is either very hard or very soft when you are cantering, and try to keep clear of stones or holes in the ground, which could cause injury to your pony.

As a novice rider, you should go hacking with an experienced person. If you are very small and not very strong it is advisable to hack on the leading rein at the beginning. In this way, your pony will be under the control of the instructor and you can concentrate on riding properly without the worry that he may dive into the hedgerows and start pulling at grass.

Bruce Davidson and J.J. Babu at Badminton, 1985.

A group of riders enjoying a hack in the countryside.

Jumping

Once you are able to ride well on the flat through all transitions (changes of pace and direction), and have some understanding of the importance of keeping your pony balanced between your leg and hand, you are ready to start learning to jump.

Ideally, you should have your first jumping lessons on an experienced jumping pony. In this way, you will not have to worry too much about the ability of the pony to jump the fence, but can concentrate on establishing a good style and the correct technique. Watch an experienced horse and rider jumping and see what both of them do at each stage of the movement. When you know what the horse does at each stage, you will have a better appreciation of what you should be doing throughout the movement. You will also see that the rider's position in the saddle is different from the general-purpose seat we have so far been working on. You must learn to perfect the forward (jumping) position before you can master jumping successfully.

One of the best ways to improve your jumping position is to walk and trot sitting forward in the saddle. When you can do this, practise walking and trotting over poles on the ground. This is an excellent introduction to jumping for you and your pony. Gradually, as your confidence and your ability increase, raise the poles from the ground, and then progress to jumping over small fences, before building courses of jumps to practise over.

It is well worth spending time and effort on establishing a secure and balanced jumping seat, partly so that you become the least possible interference to your pony, but also so that you feel secure and confident. One of the most important aspects of successful jumping is confidence, both in your own ability and also in that of your pony. Once you have established a good jumping seat, you will be able to ride the sticky jumping pony as well as the generous and trained one.

Working a horse over poles on the ground (top left) is good preparation for jump training towards either show-jumping competitions (top right) or cross-country (centre).

Jumping position

When you are jumping, you must shorten your stirrups by 75-100mm (3-4in.) from the length you have when you are riding normally. This will enable your weight to be taken forward over your knees and into the stirrup irons. If you think of your hip, knee and ankle as being rather like hinges, that can open and close, to sit in the jumping position you must close the angles in front of your hip, behind your knee and in front of your ankle. This has the effect of making your whole body shorter, and more concertinaed, and will help you to absorb the forward thrust of the pony's jump when you are in the air.

The best way to establish a good jumping position is by practice. First, try walking, trotting and cantering with this new shorter stirrup leather, just finding your balance sitting in this forward position. Later, work over poles on the ground and simple grids and try some gymnastic exercises. All this will help you to develop a seat independent of the reins and give you confidence and security.

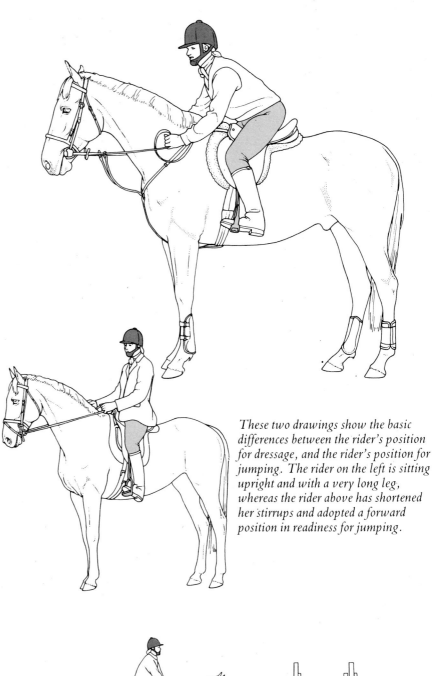

These two drawings show the basic differences between the rider's position for dressage, and the rider's position for jumping. The rider on the left is sitting upright and with a very long leg, whereas the rider above has shortened her stirrups and adopted a forward position in readiness for jumping.

1 Approach

In the approach to a fence the pony will lower his head and stretch his neck in order to assess in advance the size of the jump and the exact point in his stride for take-off. The head and neck are the pony's main balance points and he will extend them right out in front before his forelegs leave the ground. This allows him to shorten and check his final strides, and places him for his take-off.

The rider should maintain a light contact on the rein and follow the movement of the pony's head.

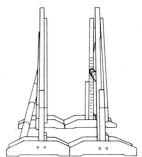

2 The take-off stride

In this very important stride, the pony will raise his neck and head just before raising his forehand. Your weight should be carried over the pony's shoulders and you should look forward, keeping your head up to help you maintain your balance. At this moment, the pony's shoulder joints open to give him the muscular force necessary to raise the forehand in the first stages of the jump. It is important that you maintain contact with the reins but still allow your pony complete freedom of his head and neck to maintain his balance. The pony's neck is extended forwards and downwards as the forelegs lift to begin the jump, and the head and neck help to lift the shoulders and forelegs over the fence.

3 Time in the air

The hindlegs of the pony are engaged forwards under his body through the hindleg joints. The 'time in the air' begins as the hind feet leave the ground and when the forelegs have cleared the fence. The pony's head and neck are raised immediately from their lowered position, to assist the pony's balance. It is very important that you keep a forward position with your seat clear of the saddle. Failure to do this will spoil the pony's jump and may cause him to flatten the fence.

4 Landing

At the moment of landing the pony uses his head and neck first to absorb the jarring to his forelegs, then to adjust his balance for the recovery and getaway strides.

5 Recovery

You should try to assume full control over your pony as soon as possible after landing to help you to get ready for the next movement.

Straighten your back and check that your seat is correct. Then adjust your feet in the stirrups and your hold on the reins.

Working over poles

Working over poles on the ground is an excellent way for you to practise your forward position: it must be developed so well that you can maintain the jumping position at the trot without losing your balance or your rhythm. It is also the best way for your pony to loosen his back and will help him to strengthen the correct muscles for jumping. Poles on the ground will encourage your pony to look down and lower his head and neck, soften his back, look at where he is going and be careful with his feet.

The shorter stirrup leather will shift your weight forward so that it is balanced deep into your heel. As we have seen, your hip, knees and ankle joints must bend so that you are able to sit forward and go with the movement.

When you are working over the poles, start with one pole on the ground, and ride first at the walk and then at the trot. Introduce a second pole about 1.3m (4ft 3in.) from the first, and a third, again 1.3m (4ft 3in.) away. At first, you

will find the trot more bouncy, and it may be difficult to follow the movement. To help you keep in balance, it is a good idea to fit a neckstrap on your pony.

There are many variations in the way that your instructor may choose to use the poles, but usually they will be placed either in a circle, or in straight lines in the school (ring), either on the track or on the centre line. It is a good idea to arrange several poles in the school, some in circles and some straight so that you can practise your position while you are moving around. Riding a circle helps keep the pony supple and alert on the curve. For you it is a good introduction to jumping, and, because it is much more difficult to stay in good balance on a circle than when riding the pony in a straight line, it will test your balance and security. When riding a circle, try to keep your head up and look forward in the direction of the line of travel. Your hands should be forward and low, taking the line of the pony's crest when you are going over the poles. In the approach and on landing, resume a light contact with the pony's mouth.

The jump seat over a small fence

When you have practised and become used to riding with the shorter stirrup leather for jumping and are more fluent and comfortable in the forward seat, you are ready to start jumping small fences. It is important that your first fences are well constructed, with a good approach and on level ground – they must be inviting to the horse. If you are learning to ride in a riding school which has a manege at least 20 x 40m (65 x 130ft), build the jump on the long side of the arena. This will enable you to ride a good approach to the fence.

Your first jump should be a single fence, either of two crossed poles or a little upright. It should not be more than 150mm (6in.) high, in fact just sufficient for your pony to canter a stride over the fence and make a small jump. Start by riding around the school or paddock in a strong forward-going trot, then progress to a controlled and balanced canter. Look at your

THE NECKSTRAP

The neckstrap is a thin leather strap which passes round the pony's neck. It is invaluable when you are learning to jump, as it fits in the correct position, and it is firm enough, for you to hold on to if you feel a little unsure about your balance. If you hold on to the reins before you are fully confident about your ability, your pony may feel your uncertainty and not respond to your aids, or, worse, you may pull at his mouth.

fence, and ride around the edge of the arena keeping your eye on the fence at all times. Ride for the middle of the jump, keeping your forward position. Your hands should just take your neckstrap, which will help you to feel safe in these first jump lessons.

When you first jump the fence, you will probably take a little while to recover and regain your balance. Before jumping another fence, you should practise cantering a large circle (20m, 65ft in diameter)

immediately after the fence so that you are able to assume complete control of your pony before you jump the fence again. If you have positioned the jump on the long side of an arena, you can practise the following exercises.

Apply your aids firmly (see page 37) and put your pony into canter, take your seat slightly out of the saddle so that you are in the jumping position, canter a 20m (65ft) circle before the jump, keeping your line of the circle and your eye on the jump.

This rider is developing a good jumping position.

Ride your circle again, then ride straight forward over the fence. When you land, ride another 20m (65ft) circle before jumping the fence again.

If this exercise goes smoothly for you two or three times, put another jump on the opposite side of the school, so that you can then ride the circle, jump the fence, recover by riding another circle and then take the second fence.

Jumping down a grid

If your exercises over one or two small, single fences go well, and you are confident in your ability and that of your pony to jump them at the trot and the canter, then you may progress to grid work. A grid is a series of obstacles, and grid work, or gymnastic jumping, is an excellent way to improve the suppleness and balance in your seat for jumping. It will also improve your pony's athletic ability and assist in the development of his correct style and technique. If you learn to jump at a school, you will probably not have to think about the training of the pony, merely about improving your own security, balance and technique. Nevertheless, all ponies, experienced or novice, will benefit from a certain amount of gymnastic work.

Start with a pole on the ground 2.75m (9ft) in front of a small cross-pole. The pole will help the pony to find the best point for his take-off and prevent him rushing at the fence. Trot, making sure that your pony is moving forward with good energetic strides, and look at the line you intend to ride. Give on the reins a little as you go over the fence so that there is no risk of you catching the pony in the mouth.

When you are confident with the pole and cross-pole, place a further fence made of cross-poles 5.5m (18ft) from the previous jump. This will enable you to enter in trot, jump the first cross-pole, take one complete canter stride (the average pony's canter stride is approximately 3-3.5m, 10-12ft) and then jump the second cross-pole. Make sure that you ride a good line for the centre of each cross-pole so that the pony meets the fences straight on and jumps them in good form. Do this exercise a few times and then let your pony rest and relax.

When you feel that you are both ready, progress to a further fence after the last cross-pole. Place this jump, also made of cross-poles, 6.5m (21ft) from the previous fence. The exercise should still be started in trot, with your pony progressing to canter after the first cross-pole.

There are many permutations of this exercise. Develop your own, sometimes using one non-jumping stride in between fences, and sometimes using two – always try to work your pony in an even rhythm so that he remains balanced. Try to fold forward in flight over the jumps, with your hands allowing the freedom of the pony's head over the fence. If you are a little nervous to start with, it is best to let your fingers take the neckstrap so that no loss of balance is apparent to your pony.

Bounce exercises

Once you and your pony are able to jump grid exercises with a single non-jumping stride, you are ready to strengthen your seat by working down grids without a non-jumping stride between the fences. Start first with one small fence, then place another fence 3.5m (11ft 6in.) away from the first – this is called a bounce fence. Approach the first fence in canter in your forward seat. Try to maintain the rhythm of the canter and look forward. Keep your legs around the pony so that you can give him an extra nudge on if you need to. There is a danger that you will grip so tightly with your knees that your lower legs will move out from the pony's sides. You must avoid this temptation – you need your legs in the correct position in case you sense that your pony

may hesitate. Make sure that your upper body folds forward and stays with the movement of the pony's jump.

It is possible to build this exercise up until you have five small jumps in a row, all 3.5m (11ft 6in.) apart.

Jumping exercises without stirrups

We saw when discussing work on the lunge (pages 40–1), how exercises without stirrups were useful for improving your basic position. The same is true with work on your jumping position: in order to improve the depth, balance and security of your seat, work over poles, small jumps and grids can be practised without your stirrups. This will enable you to follow the movements of the pony more closely and really feel the canter.

When you are jumping without stirrups, it is wise to have a neckstrap on the pony. Do remember to keep your heels down and your knees on the saddle and look forward; in this way, your seat will be stronger and you will improve the suppleness in your hips. This will help you to stay with the pony's movement over fences.

The drawings above show a rider working down a grid of fences with one canter stride between each fence.

The rider below is jumping a single spread fence from canter in very good style.

Working over a small course of fences

You are ready to start jumping a course once you can jump small fences confidently. The most important preparation to riding a course well, at all levels, is to 'walk the course'. This enables you to envisage the whole course and produce a flowing performance. We have already seen (pages 58-9) that there are five phases to a jump. You must consider four main points: the correct track to ride, creating sufficient impulsion and speed, riding accurate turns, and avoiding possible refusals.

In the approach to the fence, your pony should be in canter and facing the jump in such a way that he can gauge its height and spread, while you judge the speed of approach. Ride positively: during the pony's strides prior to take-off, your legs must be close to the pony's

sides and ready to act to encourage him on should you sense that he may refuse. Your rein contact should be light but constant, 'elastic' enough to give as the pony leaves the ground.

While the pony is in the air, you should be looking forward in the direction of travel, with your seat just clear of the saddle, your lower legs encasing the barrel of the pony and your eyes looking towards the next fence and assessing its height and distance. As the pony lands, keep looking to the next obstacle.

It is natural for the pony to lose impulsion coming out of a corner in the course, and many faults occur as a result of badly ridden corners. If your pony does lose impulsion and balance in this way, he will become 'flat' in his canter, hollow his back and trail his hindlegs so that as he

approaches the jump he fails to gain sufficient impulsion and jumps flat, possibly causing the jump to fall down.

When you first start jumping small courses, take your time and take from trot those jumps which you feel it is easier to jump from trot. It is easier to keep your balance and keep control of your pony in trot. If he is cantering, he may get a little excited and try to rush the fence. If, however, your pony lands in canter, and you feel confident, then continue in canter – returning to trot could unnecessarily confuse him and cause you both to jump the next fence poorly. Make the turns wide so that both you and your pony have time to regain your balance.

At home, practise jumping simple courses linking one fence

to another, and when you have the opportunity to ride at little shows competitively try to ride clear rounds. If you are successful in your first competition and jump clear, do not be tempted to jump faster against the clock. Riding sharp turns and jumping quickly against the clock takes a lot of practice and training and in the beginning you and your pony should aim for smooth fluent rounds. (Jumping against the clock is not usual at this level in the United States.)

It is very important to walk the course at a competition, preferably with your instructor (above). The rider on the left is jumping a spread fence; the rider on the right completes her round in a show-jumping competition.

Pony Club C test

You are ready to work towards the Pony Club C test, Riding Club grade II and their international equivalents when you can jump with confidence over simple courses. These tests are designed to examine your own personal standard of efficiency in the care of the pony and his handling (this means demonstrating to the examiner a good knowledge of the aids and how and when to apply them), and your ability to ride turns and circles, and to jump a small course. In the jumping phase of the test, you will be expected to jump fences up to 60cm (2ft) high from trot and canter, both up- and downhill, in reasonably good style.

It takes time to gain sufficient confidence to jump fences downhill, so to start with, just practise walking and trotting up- and downhill. This will make you look forward and maintain a slightly forward position in the saddle, and make you used to maintaining the same rhythm at all times. As your confidence grows, then start work in canter, again keeping the pony balanced between your leg and hand, always looking and riding forward until you feel safe and secure and your pony is able to negotiate the hills with ease.

When you first start jumping fences on the hill, make sure that they are very small – a little single cross-pole or a small upright fence about 30cm (1ft) high is enough. Begin in trot with plenty of impulsion and ride to the jump uphill first. Do this two or three times and then take the same jump downhill. When you are jumping downhill, you may find it more difficult to balance yourself so do remember to keep your head up and look forward, and use a neckstrap to help you feel more confident.

Right: A good blacksmith is essential to your pony's well-being.

It takes practice to be able to jump fences up- and downhill with confidence, but it is well worth the effort for your continued progress.

Stable management for the C test

We have already discussed most of the aspects of stable management which you will need to know at this level. We have not, however, looked at the care of your pony's feet. For the C test, you will be expected to recognize when he needs shoeing.

When you pick out (pick) your pony's feet during his daily grooming (see pages 26-7), you should also examine his shoes. Depending on the kind of work your pony is expected to do, he may need re-shoeing about every four to six weeks, but you should have a good look at his shoes every day.

1 The shoe might generally have worn. This happens much more quickly if your pony has been out on the roads, than if he has just been exercising in the field.

2 Shoes are nailed in place, and it is quite possible for the nails to be lost, or work loose. If this is not attended to, it could result in the shoe itself being lost.

3 The nail ends, which are called clenches, may have risen and be standing out from the wall of the pony's hoof. When the pony is shod, the shoe is nailed to the wall of the hoof and the clenches turned over and filed down. They can rise up, though, and stick out – this should be looked at straight away.

4 If, in spite of your care, your pony loses a front shoe when you are out on a ride, check that there are no nails still in the foot, and that the tender central part of the foot is not bruised or cut, then walk back to the stable, trying to avoid hard ground. If you cannot, then dismount, and lead your pony back.

If you start by jumping very small fences at the riding school or in your paddock at home, then when you feel safe and secure you can jump the occasional log or fallen bough when you are out hacking (trail riding). Do make sure when you are jumping natural obstacles, that you look at the take-off and landing points before presenting your pony to the obstacle as you would to a fence. It is also important to look out for holes in the ground and particularly rough going so that you do not lame your pony.

Jumping when you are out on rides is very different from jumping in the security of the riding school, so do make sure that you wear a proper hard hat with a chinstrap, and do not go out riding alone.

Competition riding

Minor competitions are held all year round. The summer season consists mainly of horse shows and gymkhanas where the schedule will include a wide variety of classes to suit all types of ponies. During the winter months, the indoor season becomes a busy circuit of dressage competitions and show-jumping (stadium jumping), again (depending on the centre) offering something to suit most ponies. It is always important to read the schedule of events carefully.

When you first want to compete, either on a pony hired from your riding school or your own animal, consult your teacher as to which classes will be best suited for you and the pony before you enter any competition. It is foolish and disappointing to enter for shows that are not suitable for your present stage of experience.

It is likely that you will be a little bewildered by all that is going on when you first visit the local horse show. Most shows – apart from the very small ones – have two or three rings, with show-jumping, showing and gymkhana events all taking place. Nevertheless, these small local shows are an excellent introduction to competing, as well as being fun to enter. When you have gained more experience, and more confidence in your ability and that of your pony – perhaps you have travelled further afield and competed against more experienced riders – you may want to use your expertise and start taking part in horse trials, or specialize in dressage or show-jumping events.

Many of the shows and jumping classes which we will describe in this chapter are organized by the local branches (chapters) of the Pony Club, and, although some are open to non-members, some are not, so it is advisable for you to become a member of your nearest branch. The Pony Club and Riding Club Movement are also the perfect introduction to competing in one-day events. Many top international riders start their careers in these events.

Riders competing at the Pony Club eventing championships. The rider on the right is doing her dressage test; the riders on the left and centre are competing in the cross-country – at the start, and jumping into water.

The gymkhana

Gymkhana events are held at many small shows. These competitions consist of games on horseback, and are tremendous fun, as well as requiring you to have complete control of your pony. Your dress need not be formal but a riding hat with chinstrap is essential as is a clean shirt, a pair of jodhpurs and boots. It is also very important that you know and understand the rules of each competition so do check them before you start. Each show will have its own selection of games, but may include some of the following.

Ride and run

Competitors start mounted and, on command, race to a given point, dismount and then run to the finish leading their pony.

Sack race

The competitors are all put in a straight line and equally spaced sacks are placed in a straight line about 30m (33yds) from the riders. On command, the riders go as quickly as possible to the sacks, dismount, get into a sack and then leading their pony, hop to the finish line.

Bending race

Again, competitors start in a line, and a row of posts is positioned at intervals in front of each rider. On command, the riders weave in and out of the posts, then either ride straight back to the start, or weave back.

Prince Philip Games (Cup)

In Great Britain, the Pony Club organizes competitions throughout the year, with regional qualifying rounds and the finalists competing at the Horse of the Year Show in October. In the United States, finalists compete at the National Horse Show in November. It is a great honour to be selected by your Pony Club branch to train to be in a Prince Philip team. The games are similar to gymkhana events, and the rules are laid down by the Pony Club.

Mark Phillips and Classic Lines.

The mounted games and gymkhana competitions can be great fun for both pony and rider.

Best turned out pony

To enter your pony in a best turned out grass- or best turned out stable-kept pony event requires a tremendous amount of hard work from you. The ponies are expected to walk and trot only, so it is a suitable class for you to enter when you first start to compete. The judge will look at the health and condition of your pony, the cleanliness of his saddle and bridle and its correct fitting, and the good repair and correct fitting of his shoes. In addition, you will be judged on your correct dress, cleanliness and general smartness. For this class the pony must be well groomed and trimmed. His tail may need pulling and his mane must be plaited (see page 76-7 – neither of these apply in this event in the United States). He must be well shod, and his feet should be oiled. His tack must fit and be perfectly clean, well oiled and supple. It must be in good repair. Avoid using coloured numnahs, girths or saddle pads. Keep your pony's dress to a snaffle or simple double bridle. A general-purpose saddle with plain girth, preferably leather, is best, though a white or plain brown girth is acceptable.

Your dress for this event should be brown leather boots with well-polished soles and uppers, beige jodphurs, white shirt, dark blue tie with small white spots and a tie pin

Above: A beautifully matched pair of ponies and riders in a pairs' showing class.

Virginia Holgate and Night Cap at Badminton 1985.

(choker), navy-blue show coat, or well-cut tweed hacking jacket, brown leather gloves and brown showing cane (this is a leather-bound cane which is shorter than a whip, and etiquette demands you carry it when you are showing your pony) and a dark blue velvet riding hat with chinstrap. In your pocket, have a clean handkerchief and a coin for the telephone in case of emergency.

The best rider competition

This class is judged entirely on your ability to ride your pony. Any horse or pony is suitable for this competition; however it is helpful if your pony is well-mannered and obedient as this will allow you to ride at your best and in good style. Best rider classes are normally very large and the competition is strong, so you must be well prepared.

You will be asked to walk, trot and canter, and then to do an individual show (this does not apply to equitation classes in the United States).

It is important to keep your show simple and short. Begin by saluting the judge. To do this, either take your reins into your left hand and drop your right hand to your side, or take your reins into your left hand and, if you have a showing cane, just raise it and nod your head to the judge. Do not forget to smile, it does help to relax you and is courteous to the judge. Begin your show by trotting in a figure of eight and then canter a figure of eight, halt and salute. This simple show allows you to be seen by the judge on both reins.

Clear round jumping

Many shows hold clear round jumping classes. Sometimes this is the first class of the day and operates for approximately one hour before the main classes start, or there may be a separate ring with a small course set up so that you can compete in the clear round throughout the day.

These competitions are exactly what the name suggests: a course of show jumps is set and every competitor who jumps clear receives a rosette (ribbon). It is a particularly good class to enter when you are just learning to compete as it gives you the opportunity to compete over a low course without the pressure of serious competition. It is also useful if your pony has a refusal in his main jumping class to be able to put him round a low course. This helps both of you to regain your confidence.

Nearly all jumping competitions are graded on the experience of the pony and his previous winnings. This is an important point to remember when you are buying a jumping pony – it is not a good idea for you to start jumping in open competitions until first you have learned to compete in novice ones. Open competitions are unrestricted so that any jumping pony, regardless of the amount of money he may have won previously, is eligible to compete. (There are no show-jumping classes for ponies in the United States.)

Polo is one of the more unusual Pony Club competitions but it encourages the riders to be competitive, and also teaches them the importance of teamwork.

Hunter trials

Hunter trials are an excellent introduction to riding cross-country. They are fun to ride and normally ponies prefer jumping small rustic fences to the coloured poles used in show-jumping, so you may find that your pony is more enthusiastic than usual. Hunter trials vary a great deal and the prize money is often high in Great Britain and the courses very large; there are, however, numerous small ones, so ask your teacher to help you select a suitable one.

When you enter a trial, walk the course on foot at least twice, better still three times. Keep the red flags on your right and the white flags on your left. Other markers such as yellow arrows are direction markers only. The start and finish will also be marked, so make a note of where they are and ensure that you do pass between them. The first time you walk the course, look for general points and walk the track you will actually ride. Note the distance between fences, and where they are in relation to each other. See if there are any trees or hedges which might help you to remember how the course is laid out when you are riding round. On the second walk round, look at each fence and decide how you intend to ride it. On the third round, try to take your teacher with you and discuss any worries that you may have about a particular obstacle.

Hunter trial schedules usually have novice (baby green), intermediate (green), open and pairs classes. The pairs class is especially helpful if you are just starting because you can link yourself with a partner who is more experienced and take a lead from the experienced pony. This will help you and your pony go round confidently. Never do more than two classes at any show: remember that two rounds of cross-country are about 5km (2-3 miles) and this is very strenuous for your pony. You must not overdo it, no matter how eager you are.

When you are riding the course, try to save your pony's energy by keeping to your forward jumping position, with your weight centred on your knees. Your seat should be clear of the saddle all the way round. This will balance both of you better, which will help you go round faster. Try to keep an even pace, and be careful to keep your pony well-balanced between your leg and hand, especially when you are going up and down hills. At the end of the course, dismount, slacken your girth, put an anti-sweat sheet on the pony and walk him until he is cool and his respiration has returned to normal. Check him for any cuts or injuries, and if there are any, wash them with salt water and sprinkle wound powder on to them.

Sponsored rides

These are becoming increasingly popular in Great Britain and elsewhere and consist of set rides, sometimes including fences and sometimes just along bridle paths. They are great fun and a means of getting to know other young horse riders in your area. A sponsored ride is normally over a distance of 15km (10 miles) or more, and it is up to you to find as many people as possible to pledge a given amount of money for every kilometre or mile that you complete. Sponsored rides are held to raise money for charity, so they are a way of doing something for people in need.

Tetrathlon

Tetrathlon competitions consist of swimming, running, riding and shooting and competitors score points for each section. The distances covered are small for younger competitors and increase as they get older. The person with the highest number of points wins. The riding phase in Great Britain is a cross-country section over fences (in the United States, stadium jumping), so practice at hunter trials will be helpful.

Polo crosse

This is a stick and ball game played on horseback, and again, it is great fun.

The stick (or crosse) has a shaft with a circular frame at the end, to which a net is attached which allows you to pick up the ball from the ground or catch it in mid-air. The ball used is made from soft sorbo rubber and is 30cm (12in.) in diameter.

You need a field where you can mark an area approximately 60 x 160m (65 x 175yds) with a goal at each end. You also need twelve riders and ponies – six to a team. The teams work in pairs and try to score goals.

Horse care for competitions

Once you start to ride more actively and begin to take part in minor competitions, it is important to consider more advanced stable management.

Trimming your pony's mane and tail will improve his appearance. Do not, however, be tempted to start trimming on your own, with only guidance from a book. Ask your teacher to show you how to do this in one of your lessons, and try to make sure that someone experienced watches your first efforts.

Pulling

The mane is normally pulled to thin out an over-thick mane, to reduce a long mane to the required length, or so that the mane lics flat. Start with the longest hairs from underneath the mane. Remove a few at a time by winding them first round your finger or a mane comb, and then pulling. Some ponies will fidget while you do this, and you may cause pain if you try to pull in very cold weather when the pony's pores are closed. It is probably better not to complete the entire mane in one session as it may make your pony's crest sore. Never pull the top hairs, nor any that stand up after plaiting (braiding), because they will form an upright fringe on the crest. Also avoid using scissors or clippers – when the mane grows back, it will look spiky and unnatural.

A tail is pulled to improve its shape and appearance and to show off the hindquarters of the pony. Tail pulling is done by plucking out the hairs, starting at the top of the tail and underneath, and working all the way down, until you get a good shape. Pull only a few hairs at a time. Do not pull the tail of a grass-kept pony – he needs the protection from the elements which his tail gives him.

Tails are seldom pulled in the United States.

Plaiting

Plaiting is something that you must learn to do well if you want to succeed in the show ring. The object of plaiting a mane is to show off the neck and head of the pony. If both are naturally good looking, small tight plaits (braids) will further enhance them. If, however, your pony's neck is straight and lacking a crest, then you can improve his appearance by clever plaiting. You can plait a mane to give it the illusion of more breadth if you brush it over to the near side and spray the top halfway down with lacquer, then brush it over to the off side before you start to plait.

The number of plaits depends on the length of your pony's crest. A short-necked pony will look better with a lot of plaits, a long-necked pony with fewer. The rule normally is to have an odd number along the mane, and one on the forelock. (In the United States, it is usual to have a lot of long plaits.)

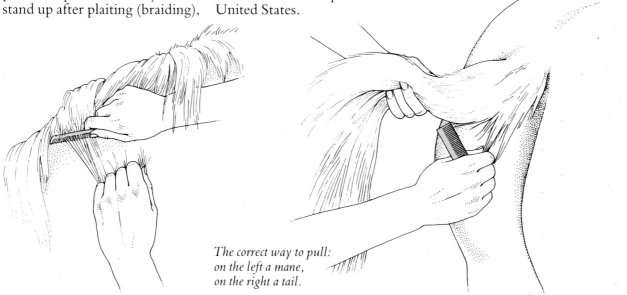

The correct way to pull: on the left a mane, on the right a tail.

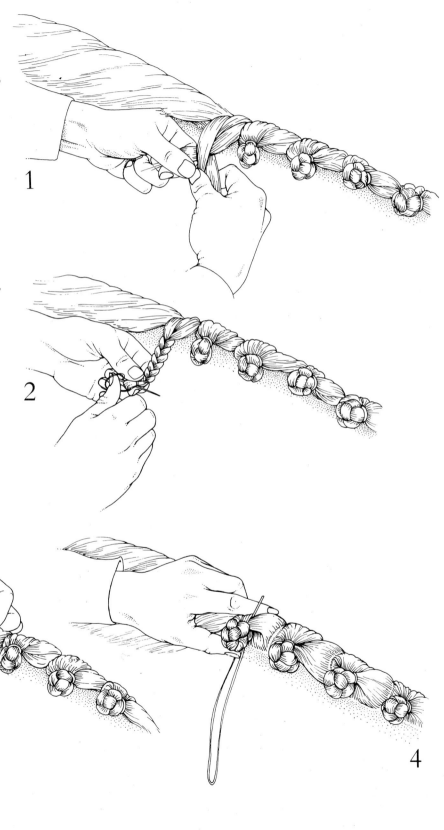

1 You may find the mane easier to plait if it is slightly damp, so brush it through with a wet brush to start with. Divide the mane into sections to make the number of plaits you require. Starting at the top of the mane, divide the hair to make the first plait into three sections and plait it.

2 Secure the ends of the plait with cotton thread.

3 Roll the plait into a neat knob and secure it by pushing the needle through the plait from underneath, near to the pony's crest, then remove the needle.

4 Finally, wind the ends of the thread around the knob, knot them underneath and snip off any spare. Continue like this all the way down the mane, then do the forelock.

Bandaging

The stable or travelling bandage (wrap) is normally 3m (10ft) long and about 12cm (5in.) wide, and made of wool, flannel or stockinette. The purpose of the stable bandage is to give warmth and protection to the limb and to encourage good circulation; it is also used when travelling for protection. Properly fitted, the stable bandage should begin just below the knee and continue down over the fetlock joint to the pony's heel.

Bandaging takes a great deal of practice and it is worth while learning to do it well. It is fun to practise on a human leg: start by bandaging a friend's leg and let them do yours. In this way you will learn to feel what it is like when a bandage is well put on with even pressure and no wrinkles!

1 It is preferable to bandage with cotton wool (absorbent cotton) or gamgee underneath the bandage to ensure that there is even pressure all the way down the leg. Start bandaging at the knee.

2 Work all the way down the leg and then back up to the middle. Never draw one part of the bandage tighter than another as this will apply an unequal amount of pressure to the limb.

3 Tie the tapes securely but not too tightly on the outside or secure the bandage with velcro.

4 Tuck the loose ends of the tapes underneath. It is important to make sure that the tapes or velcro are not tighter than the rest of the bandage, as this will be uncomfortable for your pony and could cause a swelling. In severe cases, it could damage his tendons.

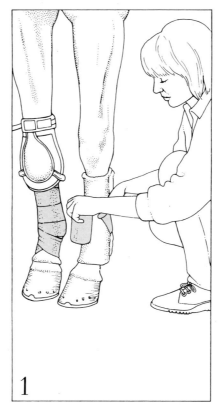

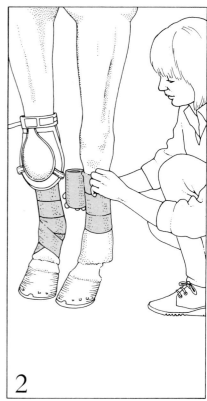

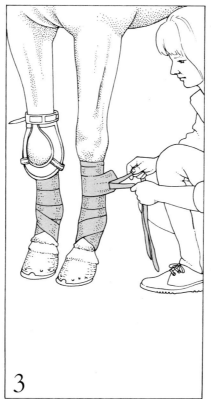

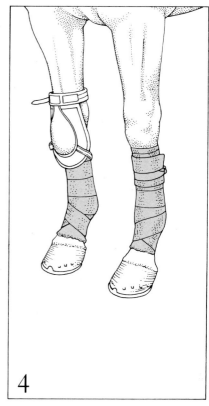

Tail bandages

Tail bandages are necessary to protect the pony's tail while he is travelling and they also help to keep the shape of a pulled tail. Tail bandages are made of crepe or elastic and should not be left on for more than six hours.

1 Brush the tail through with a damp brush, then slide the bandage under the pony's tail at the top of the dock.

2 Gradually unroll the bandage closely down the tail to the end of the dock.

3 Return to about halfway up the dock.

4 Tie the tapes on the outside and tuck the ends in. Make sure that the tapes are looser than the bandage so that you do not impair the pony's circulation.

5 Properly fitted, the bandage should be firm, but not too tight.

To remove the bandage

Stand behind your pony, a little to one side so as to avoid any risk of injury, and with both hands clasp the tail and the bandage at the top of the dock. Pull the tail bandage gently down the tail so as not to disturb the lie of the hair.

To roll up bandages for reuse

Fold the tapes neatly into the top end of the bandage and roll the tapes and bandage together firmly, using both your hands and a knee. Keep the bandage flat to avoid wrinkles.

Wash them as often as necessary – this may mean every time they are used.

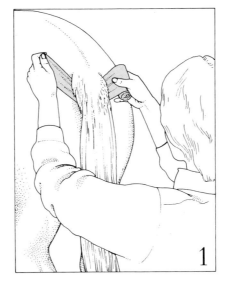

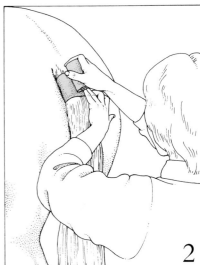

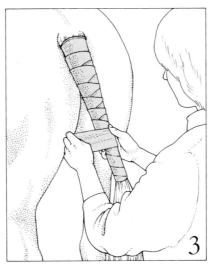

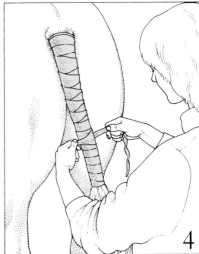

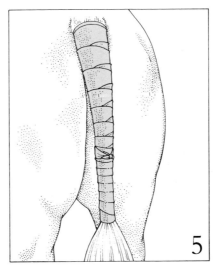

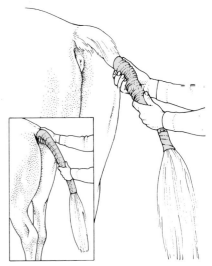

Travelling (shipping)

It is unlikely that you will be fortunate enough to have shows within hacking distance of where you keep your pony, and it will be necessary for him to travel to the competitions by horse transport. It is a good idea to practise loading your pony into a horsebox (van) several times before you need to take him to a competition – the last thing you want to worry about on the day of an event is whether you are going to have problems boxing (loading) him!

1 Position your horsebox next to a hedge or in a gateway so that there is a natural wing. Place the ramp on an incline so that the angle of entry into the box is slight.

2 Have a feed and haynet ready, and also a lunge line and someone to help you. Do not try to do this on your own; there should always be an adult present, preferably your teacher the first time.

3 Put a headcollar (halter) on your pony with a bridle on top (a lead shank over the nose). The pony should be dressed with travelling clothes consisting of a tail bandage, stable bandages, knee boots and a rug (blanket).

4 Walk your pony right inside the box, then ask your helper to shut the partition or ramp. Tie up the pony, then remove the bridle.

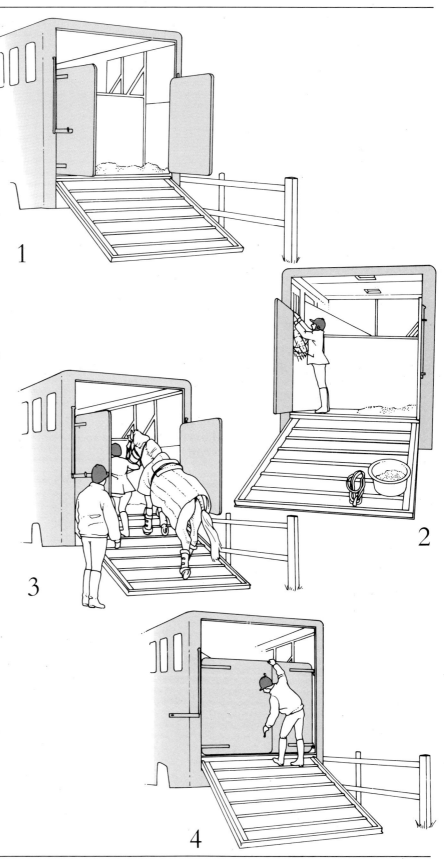

Horse trials

The one-day event, or horse trial as it is also known, consists of three important disciplines – dressage, show-jumping and cross-country.

The one-day event requires the all-round training of both horse and rider: each phase complements the others. Firstly, the pony must be trained in his basic paces to be obedient and supple so that he is able to perform the dressage test within the confines of the arena. Dressage training is the basis of the other events – good jumping depends on the pony being well trained on the flat.

The cross-country phase of the trial tests your pony's courage and speed, while the show-jumping tests his obedience and athletic ability. Many people believe that the good event horse is out of the ordinary as he is expected to be calm and obedient for dressage, bold for cross-country, and neat, athletic and careful for show-jumping.

If you wish to make progress in competition at this level, in Great Britain you must affiliate yourself and your horse to the Horse Trials Group. Similar organizations exist in other countries which hold trials. For international competitions the FEI (International Equestrian Federation) rules are followed. For all junior events (those for riders under 16 years of age), ponies must be less than 14.2 hands. If, however, you are tall for your age, and start riding horses when you are fairly young, you can enter senior competitions from the age of 14. Here, all horses must be 15 hands and over, so it is not a sport you can continue on your pony. It is often considered an advantage to ride horses young as some riders take a long time to adjust to the change from a pony stride to the bigger horse's stride. If you have talent, however, and are successful in junior events, then it is a wonderful experience and one that you should gain as much as you can from. You may be good enough to be selected to represent your country abroad in an international junior team, which is marvellous if you wish to make a career with horses.

Competing in one-day events is excellent experience even if you are sure that eventually you will want to specialize in dressage or show-jumping, rather than eventing.

This scene shows the lorry park at a horse trial. In this area, horses, riders, and their helpers, prepare for the event.

Dressage

The first phase of a one-day event is the dressage. This is the name given to the correct training of your pony, so that he understands your aids or signals clearly and finds it easy to carry you and obey your wishes. At first it is rather frightening to ride a dressage test and you will seem very alone, but it is a way of testing yourself to ensure that the work you and your teacher have been doing is progressing well, and a means of putting the training that you have been doing in front of an independent person who will judge each movement and observe your pony's way of going.

When you first start to compete, you will probably not know how long your horse will need in order to settle himself and relax for the event itself. The time that you allow for this 'riding in' depends on each individual horse or pony's temperament and experience, and your nerves! Allow at least half an hour, longer if you are unsure. This means that you must be getting on your pony 40 minutes before the time of your test, so that you can work him for half an hour, then give him a little rest and a final groom and check your own clothes so that you actually enter the arena in a relaxed manner, able to perform the best possible test.

For dressage, your pony must wear a simple snaffle bridle and

The concentration needed for the dressage competition can be seen here on the faces of both horse and rider. Precision and accuracy are two of the demands for a well-ridden dressage test.

general-purpose or dressage saddle. You should be clean and tidy, with well-polished boots, beige breeches, a shirt and tie, tweed or navy blue jacket, an approved riding hat with chinstrap, and a hairnet if your hair requires one. Your gloves should be brown. A riding whip is not allowed, but if your pony is a little lazy you can wear spurs.

It is important that you really know your test even if you are allowed to have it commanded. In the dressage phase of a one-day event, you cannot have the test commanded, but later, if you choose to specialize in dressage events – where you may ride two or more tests in a day – they may be commanded. You must know the pattern of the movements so that you can prepare well and concentrate on your pony, and not on the design of the movements. The judge will be looking to see that your pony is free and forward-going, obedient and responsive to your aids and with his impulsion or energy coming from the hindquarters.

When you are learning a test, it is a good idea to run through it on your own two feet, so that you are aware of the importance of accuracy and gain an idea of the pattern of the test. When you first start to compete, practise the test at home a few times. As you become more confident, however, it is better to work simply on improving your pony's way of going, and just link a few figures together; in this way, your pony will not begin to anticipate the movements he will be asked to do in the test.

Your entry into the arena and your halt to salute the judge are very important: this first movement can give a good impression or mar the entire test. It is well worth spending time on improving your entry, and your finish, so that you show the judge an obedient and well-mannered pony at these important stages. If you make a mistake in your test, try not to panic as you may spoil the next movement. Each movement is marked individually out of ten so if, for example, you know you have made a bad transition, try to recover quickly and concentrate on riding the next movement well.

When the competition has finished, you will be given a sheet with the judge's comments on. Do read it carefully – this is the time for reflection. Of course everyone likes to win, but if you have a good ride and feel that you and your pony have both done your best, then the result is not important. You must remember that the marks are only the opinion of that judge on that day. From the judge's comments and remarks, you will be able to see how his observations compare with the problems of which you are already aware: he may have noticed something different. If your instructor is able to accompany you and watch your test, so much the better. His comments, combined with those by the judge, will help your progress in the future.

It is usual for the organizers to allow at least half an hour between each phase of a one-day event, so after you have completed your test, check the time schedule and then prepare your pony and yourself for the cross-country phase.

SPURS

Spurs are used when a stronger, and more defined, leg aid is required. They are fitted to the rider's boot with the neck pointing downwards. If you are able to ride well and keep a still lower leg then you are ready to wear spurs; they only come into operation when you turn your heel slightly in, this is why they should not be used until your lower leg is fairly secure. It is only too easy to rub a sore place on your pony's sides with your spurs through failure to keep your lower leg still.

CORRECT

Spurs fitted correctly. Notice the good position of the rider's leg and that the heel is down.

INCORRECT

Spurs fitted with the neck pointing upwards could come into contact with the pony all the time. This is a severe way of using the spur and incorrect.

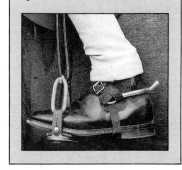

Cross-country

Experience of hunter trials is one of the best introductions to cross-country riding, so read the advice given on pages 74-5 first. If possible, walk the course the day before the competition, and then again the morning of the event. Study the plan of the course, look at all the alternative fences and decide which is the best way for you and your pony. Try to walk your course with an experienced competition rider who will help you assess the distances between fences and the correct approach to make. When you are riding cross-country, keep the red flags on your right and the white flags on your left and ride to the middle of the fences between the two flags.

Before the start of the cross-country, lay out in your horsebox your first-aid kit, two large sponges, a sweat scraper, a bucket of warm water, sweat rugs and a night rug, bandages and gamgee. Check your tack fits the pony well and stitch the headpiece of the bridle to the pony's forelock – this will prevent the bridle from coming off should you have a fall. Put leather boots, or exercise bandages with the endpieces sewn to the rest of the bandage, on all four of your pony's legs, and also fit over-reach (bell) boots. These will help to prevent him injuring himself seriously if he jumps too boldly and becomes unbalanced by stepping on himself.

Here the rider jumps the first fence on her way round the cross-country course. This rider shows good style and lots of determination.

Jumping into water can often cause problems for both horse and rider, as we can see here: the horse has made a very big jump, and the rider is not quite in balance. The rider is said to be 'hailing a cab', with one hand on the reins, and one hand high in the air.

When you are going round the course, ride positively forward at the canter. It is better to try to keep an even rhythm or a strong canter around the entire course, rather than try to go too fast until both you and your pony have done several events and become relatively experienced. If you meet any difficult or trappy combination fences, return to trot to rebalance your pony before riding strongly forward again. In the show-jumping where you are jumping on level ground it is fairly easy to judge the best pace and approach to the fences, but over undulating terrain the situation of the fences does have an enormous bearing on the pace that is good for individual problems. The experience you have gained in hunter trials will be very helpful here.

At the end of your cross-country course, dismount, slacken the girths, put an anti-sweat sheet over your pony and walk him in hand to cool him – keep walking him until his respiration rate returns to normal. Look carefully for any cuts or abrasions he may have suffered during the ride. Sponge him down with warm water, and use the sweat scraper to take out excess water and sweat from his body. Towel dry his heels, ears, and face. When he is completely dry and relaxed, put him in your horsebox and go and check the course for the show-jumping phase.

Your own dress must include an approved skullcap with a chinstrap, boots, breeches, cross-country shirt and sweater, and a stock or hunting tie. Leather gloves tend to slip when your pony becomes hot and sweaty – string- or rubber-palmed are better when it is wet.

Check your equipment and your horse's tack, then mount and take your horse for a ride around the edge of the show-ground. When he is loosened up, give him a short pipe-opener to clear his wind, then allow him to walk. Now go down to the jump warm-up area, and start first with a small fence that you can just trot over, then progress to a bigger fence at canter so that the horse has to stretch and open himself out. Just before you go to the start, ask someone on the ground – a friend or helper/groom – to check that your girth is tight, your studs secure and boots intact.

Show-jumping

The show-jumping phase of a one-day event is to test your pony's athletic ability after jumping cross-country. Show-jumping is tremendous fun and is a sport that everyone can understand easily – this probably adds to its popularity with spectators. The style of rider and pony does not count, the important thing is jumping a clear round. The penalties are four faults for a knockdown, three faults for a first refusal, and six faults for a second refusal. If your pony or horse has three refusals, you will be eliminated.

Riding a careful clear round is the result of hours of practice and training both of the pony and the rider. You must, therefore, be dedicated to putting in a great deal of hard work and effort. You must develop a good independent seat in the saddle, riding with the shorter stirrup leather so that you are able to keep perfect balance with your pony or horse and be the minimum hindrance to him. Work over small grids and combination fences (see pages 62-3) is excellent for developing this strong, independent seat.

To do well in the show-jumping phase, your pony or horse must be consistently obedient to your lightest aid, quick to respond to your legs when you are jumping and on the flat. Dressage schooling is essential if you intend to go on into open jumping classes. Courses are becoming increasingly more complicated and the related distances used demand that your pony can lengthen and shorten his stride and be obedient to instant aids without any loss of balance.

The jumps in the show-jumping phase of a one-day event will not be as big as in a pure show-jumping competition, but you should still walk the course properly. Walking a course intelligently is

When competing in a show-jumping competition, you will be faced with many different types of fence. The rider below is jumping a parallel, and the rider on the right is jumping a wall.

essential for a successful round, so when you first start to compete try to walk with your teacher or an experienced competitor who can help you appreciate some of the difficult lines and distances that may be there. The fences will be either uprights or spreads or combinations of both types. Pace out the distance between the combination fences carefully, taking into account the type of jumps used. The distances will vary slightly according to whether the jumps are a spread to a spread, a spread to an upright, or an upright to a spread. Pay attention to those fences that are not combinations but that are related to each other by six pony strides or less.

It is very important to know how many horse or pony strides there are between all the fences, and there is a simple method of working this out. Assume that one of your normal walking strides is approximately 1m (1yd). Walk from one fence to another and count your strides. If you divide your strides by four and take away one, that will give you the number of *pony strides* between the obstacles. If, for example, two fences are set in a line 20m (21yds) apart, this will give you four pony strides between the fences. (A pony's canter stride averages between 3 and 3.5m, 10 and 12 ft.)

As you become used to walking courses and watching other competitors jump, you will begin to be able to judge whether the pony's strides between jumps should be short or long. With a short stride distance, you must keep your pony very collected with his hocks engaged and his hindlegs further under his body, really paying attention to you. If the distance is long, you will have to decide if you wish to put in an extra short stride or ride with long, flowing strides, putting in fewer. A great deal depends on your individual pony and his way of jumping. The ability to decide comes with practice, with watching other horses and jumpers, and in discussion with your instructor.

Again, warm your pony up carefully for the show-jumping phase. There will usually be an area set aside for you to have a practice jump before you have to enter the arena. Put a placing pole in front of a small fence to ensure that your pony or horse is balanced and neat before he begins his round.

For the show-jumping phase, you must wear your show-jacket, with the rest of the clothing you wore for the dressage phase, and your cross-country skullcap with a black or navy blue silk or velvet cover.

Care after a competition

All competitions are very demanding and it is important that you watch carefully your pony's behaviour afterwards. It is both mentally and physically tiring for him. On returning to your stable (barn), give your pony a bucket of fresh water and make him a small feed, either mixed oats, bran, molasses and boiled barley, or make a bran mash which is easy to digest (this is not usual in the United States). Pour boiling water over half a small bucket full of bran and stir until all the bran is damp, mix in a handful of oats, plus some carrots, apples or swedes. Cover it with a cloth and leave it until it is cool enough to eat (about 20 minutes).

Your pony may break out in a sweat, usually on those areas where he did not sweat when competing. Dry his ears, throat and loins, first using hay and then the palm of your hand, rubbing in the direction of the pony's coat. Rub your pony all over in this way until he is dry. If the weather is mild, lead him in hand to help him to relax and dry. Return him to his stable (stall) and leave him with some hay to eat while you clean his tack and your boots and any other equipment you took with you. Then, put his rugs (blankets) on for the evening and leave him to relax. Check him again in about an hour.

Take special care of your pony after a competition such as a one-day event. This is a taxing ordeal for him and he should be given light work for two days after the competition before

resuming his normal work and training schedule. If the day after the competition is fine and warm, turn him out in the paddock for a couple of hours; this will help him to relax and unstiffen his limbs. Also, be careful about his feeds – he does not need as much to eat when he is not working so hard.

Care and cleaning of saddlery

It is very important that your saddlery is always clean, supple, well oiled and in good repair. Every time you clean your bridle, saddle and, in particular, the stirrup leathers, check that the stitching is not worn. It would be very unfortunate, and possibly dangerous, if a rein or stirrup leather broke while you were riding because you had not taken sufficient care. If leather is

Looking after horses also means doing chores around the yard, which could be anything from cleaning windows to sweeping down the yard.

allowed to remain dirty, it becomes hard and stiff and will break easily; it may also rub your pony and give him sores.

To clean your saddle, place it on a saddle horse and then collect together your cleaning kit. You will need a bucket of warm water, saddle soap, two sponges, a chamois leather, metal polish and rags. Remove the girth, stirrup leathers, irons and buckle guards from the saddle. Wash the saddle with warm water, using one of the sponges, and dry it with the chamois leather wrung out in warm water. With the second sponge, soap all the leather work liberally, rubbing the soap well in to keep the leather supple and soft.

If the metal parts – buckles, rings and stirrup irons – are very dirty, you should wash them before you polish them with metal polish. Rub the parts with a rag to give them a good shine.

Store your saddle on a specially designed saddle bracket, or your saddle horse.

It is helpful if you have a bridle hook to hang your bridle on for cleaning. Take the bridle to pieces and put each piece safely on a table, then wash, dry and soap the pieces separately. Wash and dry the bit. If you polish the bit with metal polish, you must wash it in very hot water afterwards so that it does not taste unpleasant in the pony's mouth. Once the bridle is clean, put it together, hang it on the hook, and go over it once more with the sponge so that it is really clean, polished and supple.

Pony Club B test

A B test candidate should be an effective rider who knows the reasons for what he or she is doing and is capable of riding over fences cross-country and show-jumping on a number of different horses. For this reason, it is a suitable test to attempt when you have had some experience of eventing. For the test, you must increase your knowledge of horsemastership. You will be expected, for example, to be sufficiently confident to care effectively for both stable- and grass-kept animals, to recognize when they are sick or lame, and be able to treat minor wounds.

If you are taking lessons at an approved riding school, then it may be possible to offer your services as a helper in return for the opportunity to help with general stable chores, and observe clipping, feeding, shoeing, and general care. If there is not a suitable school in your area and you have perhaps been having private tuition on your own pony, then ask your teacher if he or she knows of a private yard which would be prepared to allow you to help, again in return for seeing how different animals are managed.

Horse and pony health

By the time you are thinking of taking the Pony Club B test, you should be able to help out in a responsible way at the riding school where you have lessons, or, if you have your own pony or horse, you should be able to take care of him without being so dependent on adult, experienced help. You should be able, for example, to take his temperature, find his pulse, and check his respiration rate.

To take his temperature, first put a headcollar on the pony and tie him up in his stable. Shake the thermometer well down so that it reads below zero, and put a little petroleum jelly on the end. Then, lift the pony's tail with one hand, and with the other insert the thermometer into the pony's rectum. Keep hold of the end, and leave it there for just over a minute. The pony's normal temperature should be 38°C (100.5°F), although it will be slightly higher later in the day. Never take it immediately after work – it will be about one degree higher than usual for an hour or so after exercise.

You should take your pony's pulse by feeling the artery just under the jaw; the normal rate is 36-40 beats per minute. The normal respiration rate of a pony is 8-12 per minute. The best way to take a reading is to stand behind the pony and watch the rise and fall of his flanks.

Your daily care routine should alert you to any changes in your pony's outlook. Has he drunk as much water as usual? Are his droppings a good colour? Is he as plump and round as usual? Train your eye to observe your pony daily so that you notice immediately if something is not quite right. If you suspect that your pony may be unwell, call your vet. Never try to be the vet yourself – your job is to make the pony as comfortable as possible until the vet arrives, and then follow his instructions.

If your pony has to remain off work for a time, either through lameness or infection, he primarily needs peace and quiet. As he will not be able to work, however, you will also have to change his diet: too much protein and not enough exercise could cause him further illness. Reduce all his protein food, and substitute a little meadow hay, and such non-heating foods as bran, chaff and carrots. Also, give him his food damp so that it is easy to digest and not dusty.

Should your pony require tablets or powders, give them in his feed. Make the feed smaller than usual so that you can be certain he will eat it all, and make it especially attractive by adding some of his favourite food. Apples, carrots and molasses will help to disguise the taste of the medicine.

Careers
with horses

If you wish to make your career with horses, when you leave school, there are many doors open to you. If you are interested in horse care and management, taking the early BHS examinations and the stable management certificate may be sufficient to prepare you for running a stable for someone else.

If you would like the opportunity to travel and see the world, you could consider being a groom. If the idea of working with competition horses appeals to you, do not be enticed by just the glamour. The work is hard, the pay can be poor, and the hours are long and unsocial. During the competition season you can expect to be on duty all the time with just the occasional half-day break, although in the off-season you may well be able to have more rest and time away. As a groom to jumpers and eventers your main priority will be to care for the horses of the owners/riders, so that they can concentrate on training them and competing. The event groom, in particular, must really study stable management and be able to care for both sick and very fit horses confidently. This sort of work is a way of life; often you will be travelling, and sleeping in the caravan part of the horsebox (van) − not a job you can do if you do not wish to leave home!

If your main interest is dressage, you may perhaps be able to get a grooming job in return for being able to learn more, and if you are lucky, to have lessons in dressage. Trekking and holiday centres are often situated in beautiful parts of the world. The tourists are usually catered for but people are needed to ride as escort and care for the animals. This is a marvellous way of meeting people and seeing different parts of the world although this type of work is often seasonal.

Teaching in a riding school is a worthwhile career if you like people and communicate well. It is essential, however, to have qualifications for most schools.

The police force in many countries has a mounted section, and good grooms are always in demand for jockeys, show-jumpers and event riders.

Training

The first essential to starting an equestrian career is to work as hard as possible at school so that you achieve the best results you are capable of. It is important that you are articulate and able to communicate and express yourself well, particularly if you are interested in joining the police, in becoming a teacher, or working anywhere you will have to speak to the public. Once you leave school, you must decide how much time you can spend training and where your major interests lie. It is, however, always best to get a secure foundation in horsemastership and riding before you specialize in any particular sphere. In many

countries, working through the examination system to the full Instructor level will give you an all-round training as well as equipping you for a teaching career if that is what you want.

You must from the start consider how quickly it will be necessary for you to earn an income. Basically, the longer you can afford to spend training and not earning, the greater the rewards will be in the end. An excellent way of starting is to apply for a one- or two-year course on a working student basis, where you receive tuition in return for your services. This is an inexpensive way of getting your training and starting a

career. Do not take the first opening that you are offered. Apply for several posts, in both schools and private establishments. Aim to train under someone who has qualifications and is as experienced as possible so that they train you along the correct lines. If possible, talk to other students who have worked for the person you are thinking of joining. At some centres, you will have to pay for your keep and accommodation, others may offer you board and accommodation as well as tuition in return for your work. It is wise from the beginning to ask the approximate hours of

Grooms spend a large part of their day exercising the horses. If, however, you are more interested in breeding and young stock, stud work may be the career for you. On the left, a groom tests a mare before mating.

work, and approximate amount of tuition you will be offered. Working with animals is a full-time occupation, not a job or career for anyone who is not absolutely dedicated to the horse and if animals are sick, for example, you must expect to work around the clock. Having said that, it is equally possible to be used and because you are young, keen and enthusiastic to find yourself in a situation where the work seems endless and the tuition is nil. It is best to ask for a simple contract where your duties and the training that your employer offers are outlined and the hours of work, your holidays, and time off are arranged.

If you wish to gain experience much more quickly – perhaps you have already passed your Pony Club B test or Riding Club grade III – in Great Britain, you can opt to go for a short, intensive four-month course in preparation for the Stage III exam, and the Preliminary Teaching test. On an intensive fee-paying course you must expect to work very hard. Paying for an expensive course is no guarantee of success: the best teacher in the world cannot produce results if the student does not apply himself. If, however, you are prepared to work very hard at your studies and your riding, this could be the first step on the ladder for a future career. If you do pass your Assistant Instructor's examination, then use it for at least a year working under someone who is respected and knowledgeable before training towards the next grade.

The training structure in the United States is not based on the BHS system. If you think you are interested in pursuing a career with horses you should contact the US Pony Club for information and advice.

You may wish to be a competition rider yourself, but unless you are exceptionally talented, these openings are rare. Your best chance of success is if you have a little money to finance yourself in the novice grades so that you develop a good reputation making young horses. Alternatively, you could try to get a job in a dealer's yard, where they specialize in producing competition horses for sale. To do this, you must be brave and talented and prepared to work hard. As you become better known, then you may be lucky enough to ride as the second or under-rider for a good stable and gradually work your way up to number one jockey.

Examinations

If you have worked through the Pony Club and Riding Club tests, you will already have a good idea of basic training and horsemastership. These tests have been developed over a long period of years for the amateur rider or horse owner who wishes to have a measure of their own personal efficiency. Indeed, the achievement of the Pony Club A test or the Riding Club grade IV is an honour, and a very good stepping stone for anyone who wishes to embark on an equestrian career.

In Great Britain, the BHS examination structure is geared to those who leave school at 16 years of age. This system takes them progressively through all levels of instructor exams. These qualifications are widely known throughout the world and many countries have developed their own examination systems based on BHS standards.

The examination levels are:

Stage I is for the learning career student. Basic riding and simple horsemastership only are required.

Stage II is more comprehensive and at this level the career student will be becoming useful to an employer, at least in basic equitation and management.

Stage III students are asked to ride various types of horses in dressage and jumping, both show-jumping (stadium jumping) and cross-country. Their knowledge of stable management should be such that they are able to carry out daily duties with minimum supervision.

Stage IV students are all-round equestrians who know the

reasons for what they are doing, who have the ability to improve a young horse and to ride to a high standard in dressage and jumping. They should be capable of competing in one-day events and show-jumping, and Elementary level dressage (this is the third grade).

Teaching examinations are introduced at Stage III level. For the Preliminary Teaching Certificate, the student is expected to be able to take a simple class lesson, give a lead rein lesson and a lunge lesson, and also give a lecture to novice students. In Great Britain, passing the Stage III and the Preliminary Teaching test qualifies a student as a British Horse Society Assistant Instructor.

After perhaps one or two years, and further training and experience, possibly working as an assistant teacher, the student may work towards the Intermediate Instructor's Certificate. This examination is approximately halfway between the Preliminary examination and the full Instructor's Certificate, and is at the level of the Stage IV examination. Students for this are required to give a private dressage lesson, a class lesson, a jumping lesson, a lecture and a more advanced lunge lesson. On passing this examination, a student who holds the Stage IV, will become an Intermediate Instructor. At this level, a student is an asset to any riding establishment and should be able to help young students work for the early examinations, help train riders for competitions and assist in the running and management of a centre.

The army in many countries has a mounted section. Good grooming (below) produces the well turned out animals on the left.

The Instructor's Certificate is the full teaching qualification. Students must first take the stable management examination, which requires them to have a deep knowledge of horsemastership, and the ability to manage a stable, organize and train staff, and make a successful business continue to pay. The teaching and riding sections of the certificate can only be taken after stable management has been passed. Teaching and equitation are taken together, since you cannot improve the horse without the rider and the rider must ride well enough to improve the horse and be able to pass this knowledge on. The riding standard required is to Medium (the fourth) level dressage, and to Grade C show-

jumping and Novice horse trial, or US Preliminary horse trial, level.

Some BHSIs then specialize in their chosen sphere, which may perhaps be eventing, show-jumping, career training of future students, showing, or producing future competition riders. BHSIs may also work towards the Fellowship of the British Horse Society.

The FBHS is only awarded to the cream of the teachers. Fellows have not only many years' valuable experience, and all-round ability at a high level, they are also ambassadors for the Society, willing to give back to horses and the equestrian world much that they have gained themselves over many years of study, training and work.

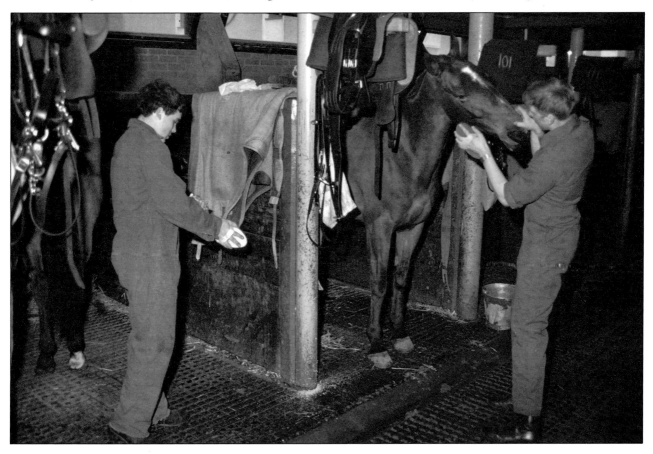

International riders

As we have seen (page 93), you must be talented, and prepared to work very hard if you wish to be a top rider yourself. Do not be discouraged, however, if you are sure that this is what you want to do – all the top international riders were beginners once.

David Green

'When I talk to other riders (Lucinda, for instance), I realize what a late starter I was. I did not start learning to ride until I was fourteen and I never went to a riding school but did all my training at home. Swift Deal, my first horse, carried me from Pony Club competitions right through to Olympic selection.

'My first major competition success came in 1978 when I competed in the Three Day Event in Sydney and came first. But I still think that riding round Badminton is the most thrilling competition a rider can take part in.

'Every day I start work at seven in the morning and train for five or six hours. Being an Australian I have, naturally, ridden in Australia, but besides that there have been competitions in America, Holland, Ireland, Germany and Britain.

'Despite the hard work I enjoy my life as a rider, especially taking part in team competitions.'

Right: Australian David Green, and (above) British eventer Lucinda Green.

Lucinda Green

'I was four when I was first put on a pony and encouraged to try to ride. I started learning how to ride properly at Mrs Skelton's riding school near where I still live, and I went there until I was ten. I enjoyed it very much and, although I was never a particularly successful junior rider, I would do anything to be able to ride! Eventually, I made the Junior Team in my final year, 1971.

'I used to admire Mary Gordon Watson and Eddie Macken very much when I was young, and I still think they are riders from whom I can learn a lot.

'Many people think that one of the greatest attractions of a riding career is the glamour – the travel, the chance to appear in films or on television, and so on. In fact, my day starts when my alarm rings at a quarter to six, and I do between four and six hours training daily: I have never been asked to appear in a film or been featured on television.

True, I have visited Holland, France, Germany, Ireland, America and Australia, but that doesn't represent much travelling when you consider it has been spread over fourteen years.

'There are times of great excitement, of course. I think one of my biggest thrills was winning Badminton for the first time, in 1973. But if you make your life with horses it is

imperative always to expect the unexpected. I could scarcely believe it when Regal Realm went lame in February, 1986, just before the World Championships in Australia. It is difficult to say what caused it, although on the previous day he had cantered around some small cross-country jumps at home and, springing enormously big over one, had landed awkwardly. Perhaps it was that that caused him to turn his ankle over and put us out of the running for the World Championships.

'All in all though, I enjoy my life as a rider very much and am always particularly pleased to compete as part of a team. That gives me a very proud, special, patriotic feeling.'

Tanya Larrigan-Robinson

'I was very lucky to have been born in the circus, where both my parents were horse trainers and riders. They had me on ponies before I could walk, so they always knew where I was! As soon as I was big enough one of my tasks was to look after a troupe of Shetlands, making sure they were spotless.

'During my junior years I did a lot of show-jumping in Britain and in America where I lived for two years. My father worked with me on my jumping and my mother sorted out the flatwork side, so I never needed to go to a riding school.

'I think my lucky break came when I was eighteen. My jumper, Indian Summer, had a back operation and was off work for about a year. My mother lent me her high-school horse, Rainbow, so that I could take part in the trials for the first Junior European Dressage Championship. Even though I had never ridden a test before, Rainbow and I made the team and my dressage career started. After that I won the Hilders Dressage Derby. It was an interesting competition because the four top placed riders in two tests had to ride each other's horses through another test to determine the leading horse and leading rider.

'To round off my junior career I won the Junior Championship in England with Indian Summer, and made the ride-off with Baroness for the Junior European Championship which to this date no-one else has done.

'When people ask me if I have a favourite horse I say that they have all been my favourites, but the ones I owe the most to are Rainbow and Salute. Rainbow taught me so much: for instance, if I gave the aid for a flying change too hard or too far back he would kick out and buck, but when I did it properly he would behave like a gentleman.

'Without Rainbow, I probably wouldn't have handled Salute the way I did as he was quite a lad. I have had ten very good years with Salute; in 1984 we finished third, sixth and fourth at the Goodwood International when everybody but me reckoned he was past his best. We also went to the Los Angeles Olympics as part of the team – that was one of my dreams realized. He is eighteen now and retired from dressage tests, but he has taken to side-saddle work so we shall carry on doing displays and competing in side-saddle competitions.

'For the future, I aim to progress higher up the ladder. Diplomat, who belongs to Mrs Ann Graham, is learning piaffe and flying changes every stride, so I hope that together we shall enter Grand Prix in 1987.'

Peter Murphy

'It seems to me that I have always ridden horses. I have certainly always wanted to be a good rider. Eddie Macken was my idol when I was young – he was so stylish and successful. Now Michael Whitaker is the rider I admire most; he has the will to win, is very patient and makes everything look very easy (when I know it is not!). My mother used to train me and drive me from show to show; she was a big help. Now I train with John Roberts.

'Working with horses and aiming to become a top class rider is very demanding. The most important thing is to see that all the horses are fit; that means giving them the right amount of jumping, roadwork, flatwork, and so on, to vary their days and keep them happy and alert.

'I travel all over Great Britain with my horses, and I have also been to Ireland, France, Germany, Belgium and Sweden. With so much travelling to shows I suppose it is inevitable that some days turn out to be complete disasters. For instance, when my sister (who was grooming for me at the time) and I arrived at the Royal Lancashire Show, we found that we had forgotten to bring all the

Peter Murphy at Wembley, 1985.

saddles and bridles! She thought that I had put them in the wagon and I thought she had. To cap it all, a driver went to collect a pony we'd been unable to fit in the wagon and when he arrived back at the show it was the wrong pony! Looking back on it now it is quite funny, but it certainly wasn't at the time!

'I love my life as a show-jumper. It is a great challenge to try to make a name for myself and earn a lot of money at it. Although I am not a professional yet I should like to be in the future. Whatever happens, horses are my life and I cannot imagine myself doing anything else.'

Carla Simmons

'I was about six years old when I first started riding, but I didn't become really hooked on it until I was nine or ten. I was very lucky because I had a super pony of my own and my friend and I used to go for lessons together. Until I was about fifteen we went to the Pony Club every Saturday morning.

'After that I spent two summers in Canada training with Colonel Michael Sutowski for the Young Riders Three Day Championship in 1983. That was my first major competition. I leased a horse and rode successfully as part of the Bermudan team.

'I decided to become a jumper rider after I had spent a year working for a hunter/jumper professional, Mr Robert Sharpe. When the year finished I didn't make up my mind straight away. I couldn't decide whether I wanted to make a career out of riding, so I took a break for a few months to give me time to think about it. Since then, I have ridden in Canada, the United States, Bermuda, Britain and Jamaica.

'Much as I love the travelling, the greatest thrill for me as a rider is working with problem horses and turning them into successes. One of my "problems" was a jumper who had a bad stop in him. I spent a year with him, training and

working, and taking him to a few shows. We didn't have much success until suddenly it was as though something clicked in his brain and we started getting placed in classes. I found that I had patience I didn't know about!

'I always try to understand a horse mentally first, to see how he works and why he does certain things. Then I work from there. All horses are different so I cannot say that I love any one horse better than the others.'

Karen Stives

'I started riding when I was seven, quite late, I suppose, compared with lots of other riders. As a junior rider I was very successful in pony and junior hunter classes, and in equitation.

'The riders I admired most were George Morris and Bill Sternkraus, although I followed the fortunes of all the top riders in dressage, show-jumping and eventing. Nowadays, the riders I really admire most are Anne Kursinski, Ginny Holgate and Mike Plumb. I have trained with Mike Plumb since 1978. Before that I used to train at the local stables and for four years I worked with Jack LeGoff as well as Mike Plumb.

'Looking back on everything that has happened, it is funny to think that the first time I managed to finish a course in an important competition seemed to me like a great success! Since then I have had the wonderful thrill of gaining a team gold medal at the 1984 Olympics.

'Being a rider is such an interesting and varied life. Most people do not like the idea of starting early in the morning, but with horses it's the only way. I start at six o'clock every morning and do five or six hours training. There is a lot of travelling involved: I have ridden in England, France, Germany, Holland, New Zealand, Bermuda and Australia. From time to time I have appeared on television, competing at Badminton, Burghley, Los Angeles and Lexington, USA.

'Competing as part of a team is a very important part of a riding career; it adds another dimension to the sport and is a terrific learning experience.

'I am very fortunate to be able to spend all my time doing what I like best. I hope in the future there will be more horses like my favourite, Ben Arthur, who is bold, independent and totally awesome!'

Karen Straker and Running Bear, Badminton 1985.

Karen Straker

'I can't remember a time when I wasn't surrounded by horses – I rode before I could walk. My mother, Mrs Elaine Straker, is an international instructor; she owned a riding school when I was young, so there was great fun with lots of horses and ponies and foreign students. She still teaches me now, although Graham Fletcher helps me with show-jumping.

'My mother says, "Success is where good management and good luck meet", and she's right! Without my good back-up team I don't suppose all my hard work would have won me so many medals. As part of the Pony Club Junior Team and Young Rider's Team, over the years I have won five gold medals and one silver.

'I really enjoy my life as a rider. It's very hard work – I normally start at seven in the morning, but if we are travelling to an event it can be much earlier than that. However, the thrills and rewards are definitely worth it. I think the most exciting thing for an eventing rider is to take part in Badminton, which I did in 1983 and 1985. It is the most daring and exciting course to ride – every fence is a challenge.

'Sometimes, unimaginable disasters happen, but you have to carry on. For instance, we rent stables at the home of Sir John Ropner where there are large iron gates. One Saturday we set off for Rudding Park Horse Trials. Mother was driving our new lorry. Unfortunately, in the hurry to leave we had not secured the side ramp and, as we drove through the gates, there was an almighty crunch. The side ramp had ripped off, but we kept going, holding the horses in as they peered out of the gaping hole. Thank goodness we had a back ramp!'

Choosing a riding school

It is essential that from the very beginning you have the best possible tuition available. The best recommendation is always word of mouth, so ask for a list of schools which are approved by your national horse society, consult your local equestrian organizations, or speak to friends who have started at a school. Visit several schools before you make a choice – most will be happy to show you round if you make an appointment. Look for ponies that are well cared for and well shod, a clean and tidy stable yard and clean saddlery that is in good repair. The staff must be friendly and pleased to meet you. Ask to see a typical lesson in progress. Enquire about the qualifications and experience of the staff, and any major achievements of the pupils or horses at the school or centre.

The facilities must include an enclosed area for beginners to start riding in safety. It is better if an indoor school is available so that you can ride all the year round, and there should be good local hacking facilities either across farmland or on bridleways, not on roads. There should be show-jumps and a dressage arena so that as you progress, the facilities will allow you to continue to improve at the same school. Ask if it is possible to work towards the Pony Club or Riding Club tests from the school, and whether they perhaps have their own grading tests – this will be a guide to whether the lessons are given on progressive lines. Find out if it is possible to have a mixture of individual and class lessons. If it is, you will have companionship and meet other young people learning at the same level, but also the opportunity to have specialized help when you need it.

Careful choice of a riding school is essential. Poor tuition is at best unhelpful, and at worst harmful, both to your progress and possibly to the animals. Always ask for a list of schools approved by your national equestrian organization before you make your final choice.

Index

Swallow Books gratefully acknowledge the assistance given to them in the production of *Riding Class* by the following people and organizations. We apologize to anyone we may have omitted to mention.
t = top; b = bottom; l = left; r = right; c = centre; i = inset
Adams Picture Library 22t, 91i; Lynne Burley/D J Murphy 88; Gerry Cranham 52; Bob Langrish 12, 98; Tim Lole/D J Murphy 38b; Peter Loughran 19, 22b, 23, 26, 28tl, bl, 29tr, c, br, 33, 37, 38t, 39, 42, 43, 44, 45, 47, 50, 56, 57, 61, 63, 64, 65, 66, 68, 69, 81, 82, 83, 84, 85, 86, 87; Mike Roberts/Only Horses 4/5, 10, 15, 20, 21, 28c, 35, 49, 53, 55, 67, 70, 72, 73, 74, 90, 92, 93, 94, 95, 101; Sporting Pictures 11, 17, 18, 36, 54, 71, 96, 99; Sally Anne Thompson/Animal Photography Ltd 8/9